THE

CAREER DISCOVERY

P R O J E C T

THE CAREER DISCOVERY PROJECT

GERALD M. STURMAN, Ph.D.

MAIN STREET BOOKS

Doubleday

New York   London   Toronto   Sydney   Auckland

A Main Street Book
PUBLISHED BY DOUBLEDAY
a division of Bantam Doubleday Dell Publishing Group, Inc.
1540 Broadway, New York, New York 10036

MAIN STREET BOOKS, DOUBLEDAY, and the portrayal of a
building with a tree are trademarks of Doubleday, a division
of Bantam Doubleday Dell Publishing Group, Inc.

Library of Congress Cataloging-in-Publication Data
Sturman, Gerald M.
  The Career Discovery Project / by Gerald M. Sturman. - 1st ed.
    p.   cm.
  "A Main Street book."
  Rev. of: If you knew who you were, you could be who you are.
  Includes bibliographical references.   1. Vocational guidance.
2. Self-evaluation.   3. Occupations —Classification.
4. Vocational interests —Testing.   5. Personality tests.
I. Sturman, Gerald M.   If you knew who you were, you could be
who you are.   II. Title.
HF381.59127   1993   92-20227
153.9'4—dc20   CIP

ISBN 0-385-42340-3

10 9 8 7 6 5

CONTENTS

PREFACE

People, as in all things in nature, are unique and grow in many directions. You are born with a set of genes unlike any others and into a family and a time in history and a place on the planet different from any other human being's. It is not surprising, therefore, that you deal differently with the world and respond to complex relationships with people and things in a way no one else does.

The One and Only You

As you grow and change, the people and things and events around you and your response to them contribute to shaping your life. At any one moment in your personal history, you are a complex and specific collection of thoughts, ideas, emotions, experiences, feelings, skills, interests, personal qualities, likes and dislikes, behavioral tendencies, personality traits, tastes, stylistic preferences, passions, aptitudes, intellectual orientations, physical coordination, and more. Some of these things are clear to you. Others may be buried under the surface of your life, unrealized and unexamined. Yet you certainly want to know yourself. As Ned Herrmann writes in *The Creative Brain* (Brain Books, 1988):

The urge to experience and define personal identity must be genetic, woven into the human DNA, because it is a driving force that has motivated people throughout all history. In the search for some understanding of themselves, some sense of who they are in the universe, human beings repeatedly ask, Who am I? Why am I the way I am? Who can I become? In what direction should I go? How can I change? Why am I here? . . . No other human being can give any one of us "The Answers." We need to find those answers for ourselves, and they seldom come fast, simple, or tidy (except maybe in retrospect). We are always "piecing it together," as long as we live.

Knowing Who You Are

What can you hope to get from a better understanding of who you are? Think of a time when you learned something new. Not just a single fact, but a whole field of knowledge or a skill—math or chemistry or English literature or American history, or a language, or a musical instrument, or how to paint a picture (or a house), or how your car works, or any other large and complex set of ideas or techniques or skills. When you first started, the task seemed massive, and each new thing was learned with some effort. It looked as if you would never be any good at it. You got discouraged, but you stayed with it for one reason or another. And then one day, in a moment of sudden renewed vitality, you discovered that the thing you were struggling with had begun to flow out of you with clarity and control. You had mastered the subject and could now begin to work with it in useful ways. You had reached a threshold of understanding that gave you power.

Power is the ability to get things done—to take action and transform undifferentiated raw material into a recognizable form. The raw materials can be physical, or they might be abstractions—ideas or symbols or emotions. Knowledge is power. When you know, you can begin to act appropriately and effectively, rather than unconsciously and blindly. With self-knowledge you are more likely to be able to achieve what you want, rather than settle for what arrives accidentally. The ability to travel to a foreign country and speak the language so that you can get what you want when you go into a store or a restaurant is satisfying and fulfilling. Fumbling around and settling for fish when you wanted to eat steak is frustrating. It leaves you feeling powerless.

Personal power is the ability to make your life the way you want it to be. People often say, "I want to be myself, I want to be who I am." But how can you be who you are, if you don't know who you are? If you don't have the knowledge, you don't have the power. And if you don't have the power, you can't get what you want.

Work and Self-expression

Think of all the different places where you say you are "working." At home, you do the dishes, clean the house, repair broken things, mow the lawn, plant flowers, paint rooms, and do all the other things that you call "working around the house." When you do these things you are contributing something of positive value to your home environment. In your community, you work on fund drives and election campaigns, give your time to the local scouts and ball clubs, and attend PTA meetings. Again, you are contributing something of value to your community. In your job, you were hired because you were expected to bring some value to your company and, either consciously or unconsciously, that is exactly what you strive to do. So, work has something to do with contributing value.

Where does that value come from? The answer comes from looking at the common denominator in all of the examples above—that is, the value comes from you, the contributor. When you say that something comes from you, you mean that it comes from your mind and body and activities. The contribution of value comes from what you do, which in turn comes from who you are. It is clear, therefore, that . . .

Work is the expression of self in the contribution of value.

When you work you are contributing value to the world. But work is a form of self-expression. Given that you spend the major portion of your life working, your experience of self-expression is enormously influenced by your worklife. Truly satisfied people are fully self-expressive. Full self-expression means being able to take what is naturally within you and transform it into something satisfying outside of you. Because self-expression is a creative process of transformation, it requires power to make it happen effectively. Fully self-expressive people are, by definition, powerful people. The world around them is the way they make it. They are the proactive, responsible, satisfied, energized masters of their own lives.

If work is about self-expression, and full self-expression is about power, and power in this context is about self-knowledge, it makes sense that the deeper your self-knowledge the more powerful and self-expressive you can be at work, and therefore the more satisfied. Unfortunately, many people are not satisfied in their worklives. When they talk about their jobs they use terms like "frustrated," "powerless," "angry," "bored"—not what you would expect to hear from people who are fully self-expressive.

To be satisfied in your job, you have to be doing work you like to do in an environment you like to be in, with the kinds of people you like to be around, interacting with the job and the environment and the people in ways that are consistent with who you are.

To know who you are and to be who you are is the ultimate form of self-expression and power. To the extent that you do know who you are, your work, career, and life choices are more likely to lead you to a fully self-expressive worklife—a life of greater satisfaction, contribution, and joy.

Acknowledgments

Experts in career development and psychological assessment have been crossing paths for years, and many have contributed across the disciplines. The importance of psychological type and the style associated with each type as indicators of appropriate career choice and of work satisfaction must be recognized by any serious worker in the career development field. Thus, a deep debt of gratitude is owed to Katharine C. Briggs and Isabel Briggs Myers for bringing us the beauty of their deep appreciation of the work of the eminent analytical psychologist Karl Jung and its application to such a wide range of human experience. The work of Consulting Psychologists Press, the Association for Psychological Type, and the Center for Applications of Psychological Type for publishing and expanding the ideas of Myers and Briggs is also acknowledged.

The career development field has its own share of skillful and creative contributors. Among those pioneers whose writings have been especially useful to the field and to this book are John L. Holland, Edgar H. Schein, and Richard N. Bolles. My own involvement in the career development field stems from a long and fruitful association with Tom Jackson and his creative contributions to our understanding of the world of work.

Additional acknowledgments are due to the Federation Employment and Guidance Service for negotiating so generously for Barry Lustig's time; to my colleague and friend Breese White, whose knowledge of career development was gained in the corporate trenches and who generously contributed his wisdom and spirit to this work; to Debbie Brown and John Duff at Doubleday, who turned my writing into readable prose; to Peter Ginsberg, my agent from Curtis Brown, who believed in the work and recognized the need for it in the market; and to my wife and partner, Peggy Bier, who supported the long hours of research and my attachment to a word processor through the many drafts with her enthusiasm for the project, commonsense approach to our work, and loving sacrifice of our valuable time together on nights and weekends.

The heart and soul of this book have been inspired by the genius and lifelong dedication of Barry Lustig, director of the Professional Development Institute at the Federation Employment and Guidance Service in New York City. Barry is a walking encyclopedia of knowledge in the career assessment field. The material selected for inclusion, the tone, and the usefulness of this book are all due to Barry's ability and commitment to the field.

Gerald M. Sturman
Bedford, New York
March 1992

1

DO PEOPLE LOVE THEIR WORK?

How many people do you know who can honestly say, "I'm really excited about my job"? Can they say it with a clear conscience? There can't be many people who can. Surveys show that up to 80 percent of the people working in this country are dissatisfied or mismatched in their jobs. It's too bad, because they put in a few thousand hours a year, and work about 100,000 hours before they retire. What a waste, what a loss, and how sad it is to spend a lifetime doing work that's not exciting or satisfying or self-expressive, or what they really want to be doing.

Job Dissatisfaction: What it is and how it is caused

But why are so many people dissatisfied at work? The clear and obvious answer is that they are not doing the job that's most natural for them. Many people don't fit in the jobs they are in. If you examine the way people get their jobs, you can see why. They come out of school, look over the field, and take the best-looking job that comes along. They think it might suit them because the pay is good, or the working conditions seem nice, or the commute is short, or the benefits are good, or a relative works there, or there's not much else around! Very few people get into the jobs they are in because they are really certain about what they want to do or know for sure what environment really suits their personality and way of working and learning, what kind of boss and colleagues they can work best with, how their skills and personal qualities can best be used to do what kinds of jobs, what skills they like to use the most, what their values are and how those determine what kinds of jobs they should be in, and so on.

So they get into these jobs more or less by accident or by the action of external factors, and the rest of their working lives follows a pattern. Put yourself in this picture for a moment:

Jobs don't seem to be "natural." You use skills you don't care about and have to wait for the weekend to use the skills that turn you on. You use your mind too much and your hands too little, or vice versa. You work in a big company when a small organization would suit you better, or you are stuck behind a desk when you would really shine if you were out meeting people. You become a manager when you are really happier in the laboratory, or you keep on doing secretarial work when you would love to be managing projects and people. You work on teams when you would rather be an individual contributor, or you try to become an entrepreneur when you really need the security of an organization. You struggle under the yoke of a big organization and a hierarchy of bosses when you would be very happy running your own business and making decisions that really count. You try to get ahead in your company but don't seem to know enough about what you have to contribute (that anyone would find useful enough) to move you up the ladder. Or you do get ahead, and as you go higher and higher you become less and less satisfied with the hours and the pace and the responsibility and the pressure; and the money and the title no longer seem to matter. Work (and life) is just not as satisfying or as fulfilling or as exciting as you had once hoped it would be. You're stuck and you're bored. You may even be desperate.

You Can Break the Pattern—the Importance of Self-assessment

This book is intended to help you break the pattern of dissatisfaction at work by allowing you to discover who you really are and how to build the most natural and satisfying worklife for yourself. Three major accomplishments will result from this assessment process:

1. You will develop a clearer understanding of your own personality type, what motivates you, and what skills you want to use in your work. This deeper self-knowledge in turn enhances your self-acceptance and self-esteem.

2. You will be able to make better-informed and more suitable job and career decisions by systematically considering the major variables related to career success and satisfaction.

3. You will gain greater insight into your developmental needs—specific areas in which you need to improve your personal and professional effectiveness—so that you can have what you want in your work and life.

Who Are You?

Four broad, basic elements define who you are in relation to your worklife:

1. *Your Motivation.* What needs, interests, values, and beliefs determine what you like to do? What is most important for you to retain in your worklife? What motivates you to do your best work? What kind of work do you really want to do, and what is it that you don't want to do? What do you want to put into your work, and what do you want to get out of it?

2. *Your Style.* How do you relate to the world? How do you like to work? What kind of work environment do you prefer? How do you communicate? How do you manage and lead others? What are the appropriate contributions for you to make to an organization? How do you relate to people, and what kinds of bosses and colleagues and subordinates do you work best around?

3. *Your Skills.* What are you able to do? What are the things that you can do that you would really like to do? What skills can you take with you wherever you go? What skills do you most want to use in your work?

The Elements of Effective Assessment

4. *Your Internal Barriers and Developmental Needs.* What is it that blocks you from getting what you want out of your worklife? What attitudes, opinions, beliefs, or behavior patterns keep you from experiencing success and satisfaction or from performing as effectively as you need to or want to? From a clear understanding of the first three elements and your internal barriers, you will be better able to derive your developmental needs. That is, what would you like to be able to do better or differently so as to make full use of your potential?

The four elements are interdependent and are interwoven in the pattern of your life and career. Each component interacts with the others. Your style is one of the determinants of your motivation and the skills you have chosen to develop. Your motivation similarly determines what skills you have developed as well as those you choose to use and perfect. Things at which you are naturally skilled contribute to your motivation, and so on.

These four basic elements, then, will tell you a lot about what you need to know to create a more effective and satisfying worklife and career. The rest will be up to you. You can go as far as you want in the career planning process, and the next to last chapter of this book suggests ways to utilize what you have learned here. To learn more about yourself and about career and life planning, a bibliography of further readings is provided in the final chapter.

The Process

Beginning with the next chapter, you will proceed through a series of inventories. Each of these inventories represents a piece of the whole—motivation, style, needs, internal barriers, and developmental needs. When you have completed the inventories, you will be instructed in the completion of a Personal Career Profile, which will allow you to gather all of the work you have done into a coherent, readable, and understandable picture of yourself in relationship to your worklife and career. This profile can then be used in whatever career planning process you choose to follow, whether it's on your own, with a professional counselor, in a workshop run by your company, or in any other type of career planning course. Self-assessment is the foundation of good career management, and your planning should not proceed until this process is complete. You will then be much clearer about your career planning needs and will be able to produce more effective results for yourself.

Discovering Who You Are

The purpose of the work you are about to do is to provide a systematic framework and tools to enable you to find out as much about yourself and your relationship to work and career as is possible in this self-assessment format. Some of what you discover here will be useful in other areas of your life. You will see the connections as you proceed.

It is important that you go through the entire process before you make any decisions about your worklife and career. The Personal Career Profile at the end of the process will help you to tie it all together. No one instrument will tell you the whole story, which is why you will use several different inventories and indicators here.

Take as much time as you need to complete the process. It does not all have to be done at a single sitting. Let your thoughts and feelings linger on some of the discoveries you make, and move on only when you feel you are ready. Set the book aside for a few days if you need to think some things over or if another project begs for your attention. Come back refreshed and ready to do more work on yourself. The experience of being in the process over several days, or even weeks, can be valuable.

Good Luck!

2

MOTIVATION

(PART 1) YOUR WORKLIFE PREFERENCES

The most important questions you need to ask yourself about your
worklife deal with what you really want. What kinds of people do you
want to have around you at work? What kinds of physical environments
do you want to work in? What do you really want to do when you're
working? What kinds of organizational cultures would you prefer? What
is most important to you? What do you really care about? What are the
attitudes and values you most want expressed in your worklife? The
answers to these questions provide a clear picture of what
motivates you at work.

What Really Matters to You?

If you want to have a satisfying worklife, you need to be in a job that matches your
answers to these questions. No one job is inherently more satisfying than another.
You have probably met people who were joyful and alive in jobs that you yourself
would find routine and unchallenging—driving a taxicab, operating an elevator,
digging ditches, waiting on tables, washing dishes, caring for babies, keeping
financial records, working in the post office, administering personnel records,
writing ad copy, working on an assembly line, sitting behind a desk, working out in
the weather, working in an office, sitting in front of a computer, lifting heavy loads,
talking on the phone all day, traveling all the time, and on and on through almost
everything that people do in their work lives. Every job is right for one person and
not for another. The real question is not whether a given job is a good job, or a bad
job, or a satisfying job—but whether the job is right and good and satisfying for
you! Does the job provide a good match for the factors that motivate you?

In this chapter, you will explore your motivation by discovering what you really
want at work in terms of people, places, jobs, and cultures—your work
environment. In the final inventory in this book you will explore your values and
needs—what you really want to get from your worklife.

The Work Environment

The major elements of any work environment include the people with whom you interact, the places, or *physical* environments, in which you spend your time, the specific work you do from day to day, and the culture of the organization (or craft, profession, or industry) in which you are working.

[✓] PEOPLE PREFERENCES

People:

The people with whom you interact on a regular basis in your work are an extremely important determinant of the overall quality of your worklife. To the extent that you could determine the personal styles of the people with whom you are going to be interacting on a regular basis, you could predict how well you would fit with the group. Under normal circumstances, it is difficult to gather this kind of information. People usually seem to behave differently when you first meet them than they do after you have known them awhile. Shy people may open up. Outgoing people may become more distant, or too friendly, or annoying. A new boss may try to make you feel comfortable at first, then turn into an unsympathetic tyrant. A sarcastic wise guy may become a trusted, thoughtful, analytic consultant.

Obviously, you can't get a psychological profile on everyone with whom you are going to work, but you can ask questions of someone in your network who knows one or more of the people in the group you are investigating. The questions need to be asked in the context of your own preferences for work associates, so you want to start by examining these. Remember to look at your preferences from the point of view of what you really value, not what you or others think is right, or better, or more appropriate for a work environment, or easier to find in the world. There is no *right* work environment—only one that works best for you. Add any other characteristics that you seek or appreciate in your colleagues at the end of the list.

"I prefer most of the people with whom I work to be . . ."

[ ] able to show their emotions and fully self-expressive

[ ] able to turn out large amounts of work day after day

[ ] active, fast-moving, and energetic

[ ] always cheerful

[ ] ambitious and hard-driving

[ ] concerned about and empathetic with me

[ ] constantly pressing toward higher levels of performance

[ ] critical and demanding of excellence from themselves and me

[ ] demanding of completion and closure

[ ] focused in their conversations on work

[ ] friendly and talkative about a wide variety of things, including subjects outside of work

[ ] helpful and companionable

[ ] highly competitive

[ ] inclined toward the intellectual

[ ] interested in company activities such as bowling and picnics

[ ] interested in cultural ideas and activities

[ ] interested in getting their own work done without a lot of interaction with others

[ ] interested in interacting with others regularly

[ ] interested in maintaining their own standards but leaving me to mine

[ ] interested in separating work and social life
[ ] interested in sports, games, and other recreational diversions
[ ] loyal to the company
[ ] mostly interested in communicating directly face-to-face
[ ] mostly interested in communicating through writing
[ ] neat and well-organized
[ ] practical and down-to-earth
[ ] quiet and deliberative
[ ] reserved
[ ] satisfied where they are
[ ] satisfied with getting their jobs done and meeting goals

[ ] skeptical and questioning
[ ] well above average in intelligence
[ ] well above average in skills
[ ] willing to leave options open until the last minute
[ ] _____
[ ] _____
[ ] _____
[ ] _____
[ ] _____
[ ] _____
[ ] _____
[ ] _____
[ ] _____
[ ] _____
[ ] _____

"I prefer my manager to be . . ."

[ ] a charismatic leader
[ ] a strong and immediate disciplinarian
[ ] ambitious and ready to move up
[ ] at my level of knowledge
[ ] critical and demanding
[ ] fiercely defensive of the department's work
[ ] friendly with the troops as a teammate
[ ] highly interactive with my work
[ ] honest and objective at all times
[ ] interactive with my work only when necessary
[ ] interested in a range of conversational topics
[ ] interested in giving feedback only at formal appraisal sessions
[ ] interested in my development
[ ] much more knowledgeable than me
[ ] openly communicative
[ ] oriented to giving me significant challenges that stretch me
[ ] ready to give feedback whenever necessary
[ ] satisfied in his or her present position
[ ] serious and concentrated on work at all times

[ ] someone who leads from behind
[ ] someone who remains apart from the employees and maintains a position of leadership and authority
[ ] someone who wants things done in a prescribed way
[ ] willing to leave my development to me
[ ] willing to let me develop at my own pace
[ ] willing to let me do things my own way as long as the results are achieved
[ ] willing to let things go until they correct themselves
[ ] _____
[ ] _____
[ ] _____
[ ] _____
[ ] _____
[ ] _____
[ ] _____
[ ] _____
[ ] _____
[ ] _____
[ ] _____
[ ] _____
[ ] _____
[ ] _____

After your preferences are clear, you will be better able to determine if you can create satisfying relationships with a particular group of people with whom you might be working, or whether you are likely to be frustrated and dissatisfied in the environment. Most work environments contain all kinds of people. It is important, therefore, that you are clear about those people with whom you would be spending the most time, or to whom you would have a direct reporting relationship.

Go back over the lists you just checked and select the five preferences for colleagues and managers that would be most important to you in having a satisfying worklife. Write them on the lines below:

PREFERRED COLLEAGUES:

1. _____
2. _____
3. _____
4. _____
5. _____

PREFERRED MANAGERS:

1. _____
2. _____
3. _____
4. _____
5. _____

[√] PLACE PREFERENCES

Places:

The physical environment in which you work is important in many ways to your well-being. Again, you need to look at your preferences. The list below doesn't include every conceivable place that a person could work, but it will start your brain working to see where it is you really prefer to be. Feel free to add any other place or any other characteristic of your preferred workplace that come to mind.

"I would be more satisfied working most of the time . . ."

[ ] indoors
[ ] outdoors
[ ] in a large, open office
[ ] in a private office
[ ] in the city
[ ] in a suburban setting
[ ] in a rural setting
[ ] in a home
[ ] in my own home
[ ] in a closed environment where I
    can concentrate on my work
[ ] in a hustling, bustling place
[ ] in a quiet, low-key place
[ ] in the same place every day
[ ] in different places all the time—
    on the road
[ ] in the United States
[ ] in another country
[ ] in a commercial office
[ ] in a laboratory
[ ] in a factory
[ ] on a ship or boat
[ ] on a farm

[ ] in a theater
[ ] in a kitchen/restaurant
[ ] in a classroom
[ ] in a retail store
[ ] in a hotel/conference center
[ ] on a construction site
[ ] on a film set
[ ] _____
[ ] _____
[ ] _____
[ ] _____
[ ] _____
[ ] _____
[ ] _____
[ ] _____
[ ] _____
[ ] _____
[ ] _____
[ ] _____
[ ] _____
[ ] _____

Go back over the list you just checked and select the five preferences for places that would be most important to you in having a satisfying worklife. Write them on the lines below:

PREFERRED PLACES:

1. _____
2. _____
3. _____
4. _____
5. _____

Job:

The job you do is distinct from the people you work with and the place you work. Your job is what you *do*. Your activities are both mental and physical, and they sometimes have an emotional content. You are not your job, the people you work with are not your job, the place where you work is not your job, and the culture in which you work is not your job. Your job is only what you do! If you can perceive that you only *do* a job and that the job part of your worklife is just that, not who you are, you can gain a vital and liberating perspective on what work is about. When you look for a new job in your own company or elsewhere, don't forget to ask the question "What will I do?" in sufficient detail so that you get a true sense of whether the prospective job is right for you or not.

To test the "job" part of your motivation, you need to ask yourself, "What do I really like to do when I am working?" The activities listed below will help you discover your likes and dislikes. They represent only a small subset of all of the possible work activities that exist or that can be invented or discovered. Add anything else you can think of or dream of that you like to do when you work that has not been included.

"What I really like to do when I work is . . ."

[ ] acquire new skills
[ ] act
[ ] act as a host/hostess
[ ] advocate positions
[ ] architectural design
[ ] attend meetings
[ ] book design
[ ] brickwork
[ ] build fine furniture
[ ] build models
[ ] build teams
[ ] buy and sell real estate
[ ] calculate taxes
[ ] calm people down
[ ] care for horses
[ ] carpentry
[ ] carry out detailed instructions
[ ] catch criminals
[ ] ceramics
[ ] classify and categorize
       information
[ ] clean cars
[ ] clean houses
[ ] climb mountains
[ ] coach sports

[ ] coach teams
[ ] collect tolls
[ ] cook
[ ] cost accounting
[ ] counsel people with substance
       abuse problems
[ ] dance
[ ] deliver sermons
[ ] deliver speeches
[ ] deliver surveys
[ ] deliver workshops
[ ] design advertising
[ ] design computer graphics
[ ] design furniture
[ ] design interiors
[ ] design landscaping
[ ] design large structures
[ ] design personnel systems
[ ] design product packaging
[ ] design surveys
[ ] design systems
[ ] design weapons
[ ] develop and print photographs
[ ] direct movies
[ ] direct stage productions

[ ] do artwork
[ ] drive a taxicab
[ ] drive automobiles
[ ] drive buses
[ ] drive trains
[ ] drive trucks
[ ] edit manuscripts
[ ] engineering design
[ ] experimental physics
[ ] explore for petroleum
[ ] finely detailed finger work
[ ] fire people
[ ] fix automobiles
[ ] fly airplanes
[ ] give personal advice
[ ] graphic design
[ ] guard people
[ ] guard property
[ ] hire people
[ ] install appliances
[ ] install computer equipment
[ ] install electronic equipment
[ ] install heavy equipment
[ ] install telecommunications
        equipment
[ ] invent gadgets
[ ] invent machinery
[ ] invent new ways of doing things
[ ] invent tools
[ ] invent weapons
[ ] investigate crimes
[ ] laboratory experiments
[ ] lead groups
[ ] lead teams
[ ] library research
[ ] locate and hire entertainment
[ ] maintain financial records
[ ] manage investments
[ ] manage people
[ ] manage real estate
[ ] mathematics
[ ] meet new people
[ ] metalwork
[ ] mine coal
[ ] move furniture
[ ] operate a mainframe computer
[ ] operate assembly machinery
[ ] operate heavy construction
        equipment
[ ] operate woodworking tools
[ ] organize events
[ ] paint houses
[ ] paint pictures
[ ] paint portraits
[ ] paint still lifes

[ ] paint walls
[ ] persuade others
[ ] plan large events
[ ] plan projects
[ ] plant landscaping
[ ] play golf
[ ] play music
[ ] play tennis
[ ] plumbing
[ ] practice medicine
[ ] preach to a congregation
[ ] produce movies
[ ] produce theater
[ ] program computers
[ ] proofread
[ ] psychological counseling
[ ] psychotherapy
[ ] purchase materials and supplies
[ ] race cars
[ ] race horses
[ ] radio astronomy
[ ] raise money
[ ] religious counseling
[ ] repair things
[ ] resolve conflicts among people
[ ] ride horses
[ ] rule on sticky issues
[ ] run a printing press
[ ] scuba dive
[ ] sculpture
[ ] sell art
[ ] sell automobiles
[ ] sell door-to-door
[ ] sell large-ticket items
[ ] sell on a retail floor
[ ] sell on the road
[ ] sell on the telephone
[ ] sell over a counter
[ ] sew
[ ] sing
[ ] solve organizational problems
[ ] speak a foreign language
[ ] stand-up comedy
[ ] stir people up
[ ] study history
[ ] study microscopic organisms
[ ] study physics
[ ] study politics
[ ] study the law
[ ] supervise factory workers
[ ] supervise others
[ ] surgery
[ ] take photographs
[ ] talk on the phone
[ ] teach acting

[ ] teach exercise
[ ] teach martial arts
[ ] teach sports
[ ] teach the elderly
[ ] teach university students
[ ] teach young people
[ ] theoretical physics
[ ] tilework
[ ] train animals
[ ] train others
[ ] translate foreign languages
[ ] type letters, memos, and reports
[ ] type manuscripts
[ ] type résumés
[ ] use a telescope
[ ] veterinary medicine
[ ] walk long distances
[ ] watercolor
[ ] wire houses
[ ] work with babies
[ ] work with young people
[ ] write advertising copy
[ ] write children's books
[ ] write computer languages
[ ] write computer system software
[ ] write in a foreign language
[ ] write jingles
[ ] write letters
[ ] write marketing copy
[ ] write memos
[ ] write music
[ ] write nonfiction books
[ ] write novels
[ ] write poetry
[ ] write public relations materials
[ ] write résumés
[ ] write scripts
[ ] write sermons
[ ] write short stories
[ ] write songs

[ ] write speeches
[ ] write textbooks
[ ] write training programs
[ ] write workbooks
[ ] zoological research
[ ] _____
[ ] _____
[ ] _____
[ ] _____
[ ] _____
[ ] _____
[ ] _____
[ ] _____
[ ] _____
[ ] _____
[ ] _____
[ ] _____
[ ] _____
[ ] _____
[ ] _____
[ ] _____
[ ] _____
[ ] _____
[ ] _____
[ ] _____
[ ] _____
[ ] _____
[ ] _____
[ ] _____
[ ] _____
[ ] _____
[ ] _____
[ ] _____
[ ] _____
[ ] _____
[ ] _____
[ ] _____
[ ] _____
[ ] _____
[ ] _____
[ ] _____
[ ] _____

Go back over the list you just checked and select the five preferences for jobs that would be most important to you in having a satisfying worklife. Write them on the lines below:

PREFERRED JOBS:

1. _____
2. _____
3. _____
4. _____
5. _____

[√] CULTURE PREFERENCES

Cultures:

Culture is defined as the concepts, habits, skills, art, institutions, etc. of a *given people in a given period*. Within a nation or a sect, culture shifts, changes, and evolves over relatively long periods of time. But in the context of a workplace, cultural changes may be sudden and dramatic. If you are working in an organization that undergoes a change of leadership, the culture of the whole organization may change. If you are working in an industry and a major technological breakthrough occurs, or a new law is introduced, or the marketplace is dramatically altered in a way that affects your industry, the culture of your organization may have to change to survive. For example, if you were working in the telecommunications industry in the early 1980s, you experienced the revolutionary changes that occurred as a result of the divestiture of AT&T. These changes have affected the industry right into the 1990s. The culture of every organization in the telecommunications industry has had to shift in order to survive and grow with these changes. AT&T is trying to switch from its traditional culture as a protected utility with an unusually large employee population and a paternalistic, service-oriented culture to being a tough, flexible, lean and mean market-driven competitor in which each employee has to be self-sufficient and responsible for both the bottom line and his or her own career.

With this caveat about cultural change in mind, you need to explore the world of organizational culture and discover what works best for you. Again, it is important to remember that there are no good or bad or wrong or right cultures, only cultures that work best for you.

"I prefer to work in a culture that is characterized as . . ."

[ ] amusing
[ ] anonymous
[ ] artistic
[ ] bookish
[ ] changing constantly
[ ] committed to abortion rights
[ ] committed to children
[ ] committed to equal rights
[ ] committed to excellence
[ ] committed to right-to-life
[ ] committed to the elderly
[ ] committed to the environment
[ ] committed to the handicapped
[ ] committed to veterans
[ ] committed to women
[ ] competitive
[ ] corporate-conservative

[ ] county government
[ ] dedicated to a cause
[ ] dedicated to making money
[ ] demanding
[ ] earthy
[ ] easygoing
[ ] educational
[ ] environmentally conscious
[ ] explorative
[ ] family-owned
[ ] fast-paced
[ ] federal government
[ ] fiercely independent
[ ] flexible
[ ] foreign
[ ] gentle
[ ] growing rapidly

[ ] hard-driving
[ ] highly exposed to the public
[ ] humorous
[ ] influential
[ ] intellectual
[ ] inventive
[ ] laissez-faire
[ ] large corporation
[ ] large government
[ ] lean and mean
[ ] literary
[ ] local
[ ] medium-sized corporation
[ ] monastic
[ ] musical
[ ] national
[ ] new and iconoclastic
[ ] not-for-profit
[ ] old and traditional
[ ] opportunistic
[ ] partnership
[ ] paternalistic
[ ] peaceful
[ ] permissive
[ ] powerful
[ ] privately owned
[ ] publicly owned
[ ] raucous
[ ] regional
[ ] rigid
[ ] rowdy
[ ] scientific
[ ] secretive
[ ] sedate
[ ] serene
[ ] serious
[ ] small and friendly
[ ] small corporation

[ ] small government
[ ] small intimate group
[ ] state government
[ ] tough
[ ] town government
[ ] underground
[ ] very stable
[ ] warlike
[ ] well-organized
[ ] worldwide
[ ] _____
[ ] _____
[ ] _____
[ ] _____
[ ] _____
[ ] _____
[ ] _____
[ ] _____
[ ] _____
[ ] _____
[ ] _____
[ ] _____
[ ] _____
[ ] _____
[ ] _____
[ ] _____
[ ] _____
[ ] _____
[ ] _____
[ ] _____
[ ] _____
[ ] _____
[ ] _____
[ ] _____
[ ] _____

Go back over the list you just checked and select the five preferences for cultures that would be most important to you in having a satisfying worklife. Write them on the lines below:

PREFERRED CULTURES:

1. _____
2. _____
3. _____
4. _____
5. _____

This first part of your motivation—your worklife preferences—defines what you really want in your work environment. In the final inventory in this book—your values and needs—you will look at what you really want to *get* from your worklife.

3

STYLE

One thing you can be sure of—you're different from everyone else.
Unless you have an identical twin, you look different from everyone else.
More importantly, you act differently.

You Are Unique

You think, talk, listen, and learn differently. You like a different collection of foods, flowers, animals, places, and music than anyone else. You have a different collection of friends and colleagues and relatives. You like to do a different set of things at work and at home and when you're out having a good time than anyone else. You relate differently. You communicate differently. You make up your mind differently. You tend to be outgoing or you're more on the reserved side. You're thoughtful or impulsive. You look at the world in a very down-to-earth, "just give me the facts" way, or you are intuitive and like to think about all the possibilities of how things might be. You have a whole set of preferences that are yours and yours alone. In short, you are a unique individual. There's no one on the planet exactly like you. There never was and never will be.

These individual differences make you special. They define your unique way of functioning in the world, and they allow you to make a unique contribution in the world.

Being Natural

This set of preferences or patterns is "naturally" yours. When you are the way you prefer to be and act the way you prefer to act, you are being natural. Your behavior and your actions feel natural to you. To be natural means to be true to your own nature.

This natural way of yours can be approximately described by a set of characteristic preferences. Taken together, these preferences define your "psychological type." Each type relates to the world differently. This manner of relating to the world is called your "style." No type or style is better than any other, as each has its own pattern of strengths and weaknesses. Though specific types tend to be drawn to certain careers, research has shown that all types and styles can be found in all careers.

Discovering Your Work Type

This inventory is designed to allow you to discover your preferred type or natural preferences in dealing with both your inner and outer worlds when you are at work. While the Myers-Briggs Type Indicator® (a registered trademark of Consulting Psychologists Press, Inc.) is a validated instrument that provides your overall psychological type across all of your life's activities, the exercise that you will do below is oriented specifically toward your working life. It is most important that you answer the questions according to the way you really behave in the work situations described. Avoid thinking about the way you *wish* you behaved, or think you *ought* to act, or think your boss would *like* you to act. Think always, "This is the way I actually behave—this is how I think, or act, or decide, or choose in this situation." Answer the questions as honestly and as objectively as possible. The closer you come to the truth about how you actually behave, the more useful the information will be to you.

Circle the letter (a) or (b) for the option that most accurately describes how you usually act, think, or feel.

1. My best ideas at work come from
    (a) an interchange of ideas and sharing with others.
    (b) quiet thought on my own.

2. When I run a meeting, I am usually
    (a) disciplined about following my prepared agenda.
    (b) flexible and open to whatever comes up.

3. When handling a subordinate's development, I am most likely to
    (a) discuss a problem I have with his or her behavior.
    (b) dislike telling him or her unpleasant things.

4. I prefer the place where I work to be
    (a) structured with clear rules and regulations.
    (b) more open-ended and laissez-faire.

5. I would rather have a supervisor with whom I have
    (a) a lot of day-by-day interaction.
    (b) only infrequent interaction.

6. I prefer meetings where most time is spent on
    (a) the application of the ideas discussed.
    (b) the ideas themselves.

7. I prefer a work environment where
    (a) frequent differences of opinion breed interesting discussions and ideas.
    (b) conflict is reduced by avoiding discussions about differences of opinion.

8. I prefer projects at work
    (a) to be well-defined and planned out.
    (b) to allow for flexible interpretation.

9. I prefer to spend my lunch hour

   (a) eating with a group.
   (b) eating alone or with one close colleague.

10. If my boss gives me a difficult task, I usually

   (a) collect as much information as possible before starting.
   (b) dive in and rely on my ability to work things out.

11. In a performance appraisal, I prefer my boss to write that I am

   (a) intelligent and reasonable.
   (b) warm and personable.

12. I prefer to

   (a) plan my workday carefully in advance.
   (b) let the day progress and see how things turn out.

13. I more often prefer to keep my office door

   (a) open.
   (b) closed.

14. When a new idea flashes into my mind, I usually

   (a) like to test it carefully before I get excited.
   (b) get excited and want to follow through quickly.

15. In a team meeting, I prefer to emphasize

   (a) an analytical discussion of the facts.
   (b) a discussion of the values involved.

16. I prefer a job in which the rewards are

   (a) seen clearly in regular periods.
   (b) stretched out over long periods of time.

17. I dress for work

   (a) so that other people notice and admire my clothing.
   (b) in a way that blends in with the norm.

18. When I solve problems, I am more likely to

   (a) give most weight to the facts in front of me.
   (b) explore the full range of possibilities.

19. If I have to confront colleagues or subordinates, I am usually

   (a) interested in making sure I give them the facts accurately.
   (b) more interested in making sure I don't hurt their feelings.

20. I would rather have a boss who

   (a) provides a lot of structure and organization.
   (b) leaves me to do things however they work best for me.

21. I prefer most of my jobs at work to be

   (a) a continuing series of short tasks.
   (b) long projects on which I can concentrate my efforts.

22. When I write a report, I usually think first of
    (a) the details.
    (b) the big picture.

23. When I have a decision to make at work, I usually
    (a) reason it through regardless of my feelings.
    (b) consider my feelings to be very important.

24. I prefer my own office to be one in which
    (a) things are orderly, organized, and systematic.
    (b) there is a creative array of projects, papers, and books.

25. When I have lunch with my colleagues, I would rather
    (a) talk about people.
    (b) talk about ideas.

26. I would rather have my boss trust me with
    (a) practical problems to solve.
    (b) policy problems to solve.

27. When faced with a decision at work, I usually prefer to
    (a) think things through.
    (b) trust my gut feelings.

28. I prefer the work I do every day to
    (a) be continuous and relatively predictable.
    (b) have frequent changes in activities and schedules.

29. When I have to organize and run a meeting, I more often
    (a) feel satisfied that I have the opportunity to lead.
    (b) prefer that someone else had the responsibility.

30. If I were asked to prepare a strategic plan, I would be more likely to
    (a) emphasize what is practical now.
    (b) orient the plan toward future possibilities.

31. When faced with a decision at work, I usually
    (a) focus on the facts and figures above all.
    (b) give careful attention to people's feelings.

32. When my boss gives me a new project, I usually prefer
    (a) a clear statement of what is expected.
    (b) to be left to work it out the way I want.

33. I prefer to have
    (a) a large group of colleagues at work.
    (b) a few colleagues that I know well.

34. In one-on-one meetings, I am more likely to
    (a) listen quietly and absorb details.
    (b) anticipate the speaker's words and interject.

35. If someone argues with a policy or decision I make, I usually

   (a) remain firm.
   (b) seek to avoid unpleasantness, anger, and disharmony.

36. When I have made a tough choice at work, I usually

   (a) am satisfied that it is done.
   (b) wish that I could remain open to other alternatives.

37. When I attend a company outing, I usually

   (a) walk around and meet people I may not know well.
   (b) hang out with the colleagues I know best.

38. I think my colleagues see me more

   (a) as a here-and-now person.
   (b) as someone with an orientation toward the future.

39. When I have a long and complex report to read, I am more likely to

   (a) be patient and study the details.
   (b) try to get the general ideas and see how I feel about them.

40. I prefer my work environment to be

   (a) comfortable, predictable, and stable.
   (b) flexible and changing.

41. My colleagues at work are more likely to describe me as

   (a) an energetic team player.
   (b) a quiet and thoughtful employee.

42. When I prepare a presentation, I prefer to emphasize

   (a) the use of real facts from my own experience.
   (b) the discussion of ideas and concepts.

43. I prefer to work with colleagues who

   (a) rely heavily on logic.
   (b) look more often to their feelings.

44. If someone on my team is late with a scheduled task, I usually

   (a) get impatient and annoyed.
   (b) look for ways to stretch the deadlines.

45. When I attend a training session, I am more likely to

   (a) participate openly and actively.
   (b) let others take the active role.

46. When colleagues and subordinates present ideas to me, I am usually more interested in

   (a) immediately useful ideas.
   (b) ideas with innovative approaches.

47. If I have to deal with a colleague's feelings, I prefer to be

   (a) truthful even if I can't be tactful.
   (b) tactful, even if I can't tell the truth.

48. I prefer projects that
   (a) have a clear ending date when I know they will be finished.
   (b) may remain open-ended to ensure that all bases are covered.

49. When I have a decision to make at work, I more often
   (a) talk it over with a number of people before I decide.
   (b) spend most of my time working it out in my own head.

50. I prefer a job where I can
   (a) use my experience to work at familiar tasks.
   (b) confront ideas and problems that are new to me.

51. When I am at a meeting and a difference of opinion gets heated, I usually
   (a) defend the side I think is most logical.
   (b) try to create a harmonious atmosphere and solution.

52. When I get a new project, I usually prefer to
   (a) get to it and complete it as quickly as possible.
   (b) move as slowly as allowable and explore various approaches.

53. I am more interested in
   (a) the actual tasks I am doing day-by-day.
   (b) the thoughts I have about my work.

54. When I attend a training session, I usually prefer
   (a) experiential processes.
   (b) information and abstractions.

55. When I have a meeting with a colleague, I usually
   (a) get through it quickly in a businesslike manner.
   (b) linger over the sociable interaction.

56. I would rather be in a job with
   (a) activities requiring me to reach a conclusion.
   (b) activities that allow me to stay open to my experience.

57. When I ask a colleague for advice or help, I am usually
   (a) comfortable.
   (b) somewhat ill at ease.

58. In a meeting or when reading a report, I am more likely to
   (a) remember the facts presented.
   (b) remember mostly the concepts presented.

59. When colleagues ask my advice about a work matter, I more often
   (a) guide them toward a decision based purely on logic.
   (b) help them explore the values and policies in the situation.

60. When I am in a meeting, I am usually more interested in
   (a) getting the job done as quickly as possible.
   (b) spending time making sure everyone gets heard.

61. When I am interrupted in the middle of a tough job, I usually

   (a) welcome the opportunity to talk to someone.
   (b) prefer to be left alone with my thoughts.

62. When I read a report, I usually go first to

   (a) the body of detailed information.
   (b) the summary or executive overview.

63. When I am putting forward a new idea at work, I more often

   (a) remain firm about the correctness of it.
   (b) try to persuade others by appealing to their sense of value.

64. If my boss insists that I schedule my workday, I feel

   (a) satisfied I am organized.
   (b) uncomfortable that I am constrained.

65. When I am at a meeting and someone tells a joke, I usually

   (a) laugh and think of one to tell.
   (b) enjoy the joke quietly.

66. In a performance appraisal, it would be more accurate if my boss said I was

   (a) practical.
   (b) imaginative.

67. I am usually more interested in how my colleagues

   (a) think about problems.
   (b) feel about problems.

68. When a new and unusual policy announcement is issued at work, I am usually

   (a) annoyed or otherwise upset at the changes.
   (b) interested in seeing how I will handle the new environment.

69. In a meeting, I usually

   (a) speak out directly when I want to.
   (b) wait until I am asked directly before I speak.

70. When I start a new project, I usually

   (a) write a step-by-step plan early in the process.
   (b) wait and see how things develop before planning.

71. When I hear a presentation from a colleague, I am more likely to be

   (a) openly and intellectually critical.
   (b) careful in voicing my opinions, especially when I disagree.

72. If they couldn't be both, I would rather have colleagues who are

   (a) well-organized.
   (b) spontaneous.

73. I would prefer to work in a company where

   (a) everyone works together in an open, active environment.
   (b) people work independently in their own spaces.

74. I more often seek out work that applies
    (a) my practical skills and nature.
    (b) my ability to create new ideas and things.

75. When I have to make a decision at work, I am more likely to
    (a) analyze the situation logically without considering my values and feelings.
    (b) put a strong emphasis on applying my values and feelings to the solution.

76. When I present my views in a meeting, I am usually
    (a) decisive.
    (b) open to having others suggest changes and other views.

77. When I need to pass on an idea or information, I prefer to
    (a) talk directly to people about it.
    (b) put it in writing.

78. My leadership style is best described as
    (a) practical.
    (b) visionary.

79. In a performance appraisal meeting, I am usually more likely to
    (a) be frank and honest regardless of feelings.
    (b) try to smooth over any problems and avoid hurt feelings.

80. When I am discussing an important issue at a meeting, I usually
    (a) try to reach a definite conclusion quickly.
    (b) keep the options open.

81. I enjoy more
    (a) a workday filled with variety and interactions with others.
    (b) working without interacting with others for long periods of time.

82. I prefer a work situation that is
    (a) stable with little change.
    (b) full of change.

83. My colleagues would be more likely to describe my behavior at work as
    (a) cool, calm, and objective.
    (b) warm and feeling.

84. At work, I prefer projects
    (a) on which I work quickly to make a short deadline.
    (b) that have longer and more flexible deadlines.

85. When I am in a meeting with colleagues and a high-ranking manager or executive comes in, I usually
    (a) greet the person in a comfortable and friendly way.
    (b) wait until I see how others react to him or her.

86. When I think of my most important work assets, they are
    (a) more in the realm of the practical.
    (b) more inclined toward the realm of ideas.

87. In a training session or course, I prefer a trainer who depends more on
    (a) precision and logic.
    (b) emotion and experience.

88. I usually push my colleagues or subordinates for
    (a) quick decisions.
    (b) thorough review, even at the risk of delaying decisions.

Scoring Your Work Type

On the Type Scoring Form on the following page, check the (a) or (b) box corresponding to your answer for each question. Add up the checks in each column. The larger score of each pair corresponds to a letter indicating your type preference in four categories. Write the four letters in the spaces provided below:

My Type is: _____ _____ _____ _____

Now proceed to the pages following the scoring form for an explanation of the type preferences and a description of the style with which each type relates to the world.

Type Scoring Form

	a	b		a	b		a	b		a	b
1			2			3			4		
5			6			7			8		
9			10			11			12		
13			14			15			16		
17			18			19			20		
21			22			23			24		
25			26			27			28		
29			30			31			32		
33			34			35			36		
37			38			39			40		
41			42			43			44		
45			46			47			48		
49			50			51			52		
53			54			55			56		
57			58			59			60		
61			62			63			64		
65			66			67			68		
69			70			71			72		
73			74			75			76		
77			78			79			80		
81			82			83			84		
85			86			87			88		

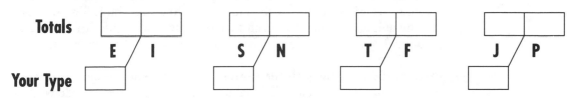

Totals

E / I   S / N   T / F   J / P

Your Type

Work Type

The four-letter work type you just discovered identifies a set of preferences that determines your work style. Each work type identifies a different work style.

The notion of preferences and their effect on style was first developed by the psychologist Carl Jung. In order to make Jung's work more accessible to people and useful in self-understanding, Isabel Briggs Myers and Katharine C. Briggs devised the Myers-Briggs Type Indicator® (MBTI®). They described four indicators of an individual's type.

1. **Extroversion-Introversion.** This indicator refers to an individual's preference for extroversion (E) or introversion (I). Extroverts are primarily activity-oriented, with a keen awareness of the external world. They tend to look outside of themselves and derive much of their energy from interacting with others. Introverts, on the other hand, tend to look inward to the world of ideas and are most comfortable in thoughtful contemplation, energized by the workings of their own inner world.

2. **Perception.** The second indicator refers to the two ways people have of perceiving the world and taking in information—through sensing (S) with the five senses or through intuition (N), which is the process of perceiving the world through meanings and relationships that cannot be seen, heard, smelled, tasted, or felt. People who prefer sensing are more interested in what is actually in their immediate environment. They tend to perceive the world at large in a more factual, concrete, and specific way. Intuitive people tend to read between the lines and look for the possibilities in things rather than concentrating on the things themselves. They tend to take a more global, "big picture" view of things.

3. **Judgment.** The third indicator refers to the two ways people have of reaching conclusions about what they have perceived—thinking (T), in which conclusions are based on logical, objective processes, or feeling (F), in which conclusions are made more subjectively and on the basis of personal values. The person who prefers thinking will judge things according to their consistency and logic. The thinking person uses reasoning power to make judgments about things. The person who prefers feeling is more likely to judge things according to his own sense of values.

   It is important not to confuse "judging" with being "judgmental." "Judgmental" means to be critical or to criticize everything. "To judge" means to come to an opinion about something. It is also important not to confuse "feeling" as it is used here with "emotion." To prefer the feeling process for making judgments does not mean that an individual decides things in an emotional way. "Feeling" refers here to values rather than emotions.

4. **Process for Dealing with the Outer World.** The final indicator refers to the preferred process that an individual uses in relating to the outside world—judgment (J), in which the outer world is dealt with principally through one of the two judgment processes, thinking or feeling, or perception (P), in which the outside world is dealt with principally through one of the two perceiving processes, sensing or intuition. People who approach life and the world primarily through judgment like to bring things to completion in their lives.

They seek organization and structure. They prefer to make conclusive decisions and then shut off the perceiving process in order to avoid confusion. Those who favor the perceiving process, on the other hand, like to keep things open and flowing, and tend to delay making decisions to allow further evidence to keep coming in. They generally approach life in a more open-ended, flexible, less structured manner.

Your Work Type

There are sixteen possible combinations of the four preferences. Each of these combinations represents a distinct work type with a style different in many characteristics from each of the others. When reading through these style descriptions, it is important to remember the following caveats:

1. Your behavior is unlikely to be exactly consistent with the style description of your work type. These descriptions are broad and are meant to demonstrate inclinations toward certain behavior rather than to be precise descriptions of how you would behave in *every* situation. There is no such thing as a "pure type."

2. You need not rely exclusively on the assessment score to determine your type and its style. If the score for the two pairs in any of the dimensions was close and you are uncertain about which you really are, read the style descriptions for both of the types and see which fits you better (for example, if you are uncertain whether you are an ENTJ or an ESTJ because your S and N scores were close, read the descriptions for both ENTJ and ESTJ).

3. No one type or style is better than any other—only different! The world needs every work type, and a wide variety of types can be found in almost every organization, family, team, or other collection of human beings. In addition, you use all of the functions and express many of the attitudes at different times. Your type only indicates those you most prefer. Types are complementary, and every group benefits from a variety of work types. Extroverts need introverts, sensing types need intuitive types, thinkers need feelers, and people who process the world through their judgments need people around them who process the world through their perceptions.

Style Descriptions of the Work Types

The style descriptions are located on the following pages:

[√]   I S T J

Analytical Manager of Facts and Details

Profile:

ISTJs are characterized as serious and quiet. They become successful through their ability to concentrate and perform tasks in a thorough manner. They are practical, logical, dependable, orderly, matter-of-fact, and well-organized. They are not easily distracted and make up their own minds about how a job should be accomplished regardless of outside protest or interference. They pay great attention to details and operate well in stable environments. They do not like things that are frivolous or new, and are patient and sensible.

Attributes:

Conservative, decisive, dependable, duty-bound, factual, organized, painstaking, practical, realistic, reliable, sensible, stable, steadfast, systematic, thorough.

Preferred Work Environment

They prefer to work in a structured, orderly, task-oriented environment that allows them to work independently and privately so that their work can be uninterrupted. They like organizations in which they have a good measure of security that will provide rewards for their steady work. They like their colleagues to be as hard-working as they are and to be interested in producing results from an analysis of the facts.

Interpersonal Style:

These people readily accept responsibility and are well-organized. When they serve in leading administrative positions, they produce a stabilizing influence and show good judgment and a memory for details. When their own needs have been firmly established, they are able to respect the needs of others.

Possible Developmental Needs:

These people sometimes need to develop a deeper understanding of their colleagues and coworkers. It is particularly valuable for them to learn to acknowledge others openly. They may need to give more attention to organizing the way they deal with the outer world and to avoid becoming too preoccupied with their inner life. Attempting new approaches can keep them from getting stuck in monotonous routine.

[√] I S F J

Sympathetic Manager of Facts and Details

Profile:

These people live their lives in a style that is quiet, responsible, and conscientious, and are generally friendly. They work hard to carry out their responsibilities and to serve their friends and coworkers. They are thorough and work accurately. They are patient in dealing with details and routine, and need time to master technical material. They are loyal and considerate of the feelings of others. Dedicated and service-oriented individuals, they are dependable, orderly, and responsive to the needs of others.

Attributes:

Conscientious, conservative, dependable, detailed, devoted, helpful, loyal, meticulous, orderly, organized, painstaking, patient, practical, protective, responsible, service-minded, stable, sympathetic, systematic, traditional.

Preferred Work Environment:

They like a calm, orderly, and quiet environment with privacy to work efficiently. They seek security and a clearly strutured way of working. They prefer colleagues who work diligently on well-structured tasks. They like to provide practical services to people.

Interpersonal Style:

Characterized as "people people," they are loyal, supportive, considerate, sympathetic, and helpful. They communicate with genuine personal warmth and work hard to keep their word in dealing with friends. They are naturally drawn to modest, quiet people.

Possible Developmental Needs:

They may need to develop a more direct and assertive, and at times a more positive and optimistic, approach to the world. It may also be helpful to develop an understanding of their own true value. Some may need to learn to delegate more to others and not overwork themselves. They should be prepared to take the time required to master technical subjects when necessary.

[√] INFJ

People-Oriented Innovator of Ideas

Profile:

These people achieve their success through perseverance, originality, and the motivation to do whatever is required. Putting their full selves and best effort into their work, they frequently show themselves to be innovators of new ideas. Quietly forceful, conscientious, concerned for other, they are respected for their firm principles. Their intuition is strong, generating a good deal of inspiration. This in turn is important to them. They are likely to be honored for their leadership, winning others by their ideas rather than demanding cooperation or support.

Attributes:

Committed, compassionate, conceptual, concerned, creative, deep, determined, empathetic, forceful, holistic, idealistic, intense, loyal, persevering, reserved, sensitive, serious.

Preferred Work Environment:

These people prefer a warm, human-oriented environment that allows time for quiet contemplation and opportunities to demonstrate creativity. Colleagues will be harmonious individuals committed to improving the world and supporting the well-being of others.

Interpersonal Style:

Highly empathetic in their dealings with others, they nevertheless earn respect for maintaining firm principles. They usually have a strong, long-term, inner circle of friends and share their feelings only after developing deep trust. They get along well with complex individuals and are sensitive to their emotions and personal interests. They acknowledge others naturally and easily win their support.

Possible Developmental Needs:

They may need to become more active in both giving and accepting constructive criticism, rather than seeking harmony above all. Ideas that conflict with their values should be reviewed for merit rather than dismissed out of hand. They need to consider a full range of facts, figures, and problems and avoid a single-minded concentration on personal vision.

[√] INTJ

Logical, Critical, Decisive Innovator of Ideas

Profile:

Marked by original minds and relentless innovation in thought as well as action, they are particularly turned on by very difficult problems. Their strong faith in their own intuitive power makes them unusually successful problem-solvers. Characterized as skeptical, critical, independent, determined, and stubborn, they have the most independent style of all of the types. They are skilled at building systems and products by means of logic and theory. INTJs place a high value on their own competence as well as that of others and will therefore drive others just as hard as they drive themselves.

Attributes:

Autonomous, critical, decisive, demanding, firm, global, independent, individualistic, inspirational, logical, original, private, serious, systems-oriented, theoretical, visionary.

Preferred Work Environment:

These people prefer autonomy in their work and want privacy for thoughtful contemplation. They also prefer opportunities for expressing their creativity. They prize efficiency and colleagues who are intellectually stimulating, productive, effective, and committed to dealing with long-range issues consistent with the INTJ's vision of the future.

Interpersonal Style:

These are the hard-driving, independent, individualistic people who remain determined and decisive regardless of external conditions or the agendas of others. They are oblivious to criticism and indifference alike and are often characterized as unyielding.

Possible Developmental Needs:

They may need to analyze their own ideas more carefully and develop a more realistic approach in order to bring projects to fruition. It might be helpful to be more open and less stubborn when others present ideas. They may need to realize that a project requires care and activity throughout its life cycle and not only during the creative stages. They may need to pay more attention to how their behavior affects other people.

[√] ISTP

Practical Analyzer

Profile:

These people may be characterized as "cool onlookers." They are quiet and reserved, and observe and analyze life with a detached curiosity and unexpected flashes of original humor. They are logical, analytical, and unlikely to be swayed by anything but a well-reasoned argument based on solid facts. They are action-oriented, precise, and tireless, but will avoid inefficient waste of time and energy. They show a strong interest in the inner workings of things and are likely to excel in the applied sciences and engineering. Socially, they may appear shy with all but their closest friends or relations.

Attributes:

Adaptable, adventurous, analytical, applied, curious, expedient, factual, independent, logical, observant, practical, realistic, reflective, self-determined, spontaneous.

Preferred Work Environment:

These people prefer an action-oriented environment among people who are focused on solving immediate problems. They like to be free to operate independently with few organizational constraints, rules, and regulations. They prefer projects on which they can have hands-on participation.

Interpersonal Style:

Although they tend toward shyness, they are action-oriented and prefer to demonstrate their views by example. They like to communicate directly and generally "tell it like they see it." They are loyal and generous in their relationships.

Possible Developmental Needs:

They may need to recognize the purpose for authority and curb a tendency toward insubordination. It may be important to work on planning skills, goal-setting, and developing perseverance in the achievement of well-defined targets. They may need to become more open to the feelings and needs of others.

[√] ISFP

Observant, Loyal Helper

Profile:
Characterized by a modest, retiring, and quietly friendly face to the world, these people seldom display the warmth that exists abundantly inside. They avoid disagreements, yet stick to their values with passionate conviction. They are usually reluctant to lead but can make passionate followers. They are tolerant, flexible, open-minded, and adaptable, and seek simplicity and freedom. They digest experience deeply and stubbornly maintain their loyalties. They do not seek to dominate or impress others, but value most those who try to understand their goals and inner beliefs. They live well in the moment and take their time about getting things done.

Attributes:
Adaptable, caring, cooperative, empathetic, flexible, gentle, harmonious, loyal, modest, observant, patient, realistic, reflective, retiring, sensitive, spontaneous, trusting, understanding.

Preferred Work Environment:
These people like to be in a compatible, harmonious, people-oriented situation working with colleagues who go about their business quietly and courteously and take pleasure in their work. The environment should be attractive and allow for some flexibility and a private place to work.

Interpersonal Style:
These people are good team players who accept direction from leaders. They do not spend time judging others, and have little need to dominate. They work best with people who are sympathetic to and understand their goals. They seek to persuade and motivate others through praise and loyalty rather than criticism.

Possible Developmental Needs:
It may be important for them to develop a more assertive approach to their work, develop a slightly more skeptical attitude, and learn to analyze rather than accept things outright. They may need to learn to take feedback without being overly sensitive, learn to appreciate their own accomplishments more, and give constructive criticism to others. They may need to take a broader view, become more future-oriented, curb their impulses, and organize their time and resources in advance.

[√] INFP

Imaginative, Independent Helper

Profile:

Enthusiastic and loyal people, but not obtrusively so except among close colleagues and friends. Their deepest feelings are seldom expressed; their inner tenderness is masked by a quiet reserve. INFPs care about learning, ideas, and language, and enjoy developing independent projects of their own. Their main strength lies in an intuitive sense of the possible, beyond the obvious or easily seen facts presently at hand. They work best when they have a mission and sometimes undertake heavy responsibilities in such conditions. They can be characterized as flexible, tolerant, and open-minded.

Attributes:

Adaptable, committed, compassionate, creative, curious, deep, devoted, empathetic, gentle, imaginative, independent, inquisitive, loyal, reticent, virtuous.

Preferred Work Environment:

These people prefer to work with others who share similar values and are committed to people-related issues. They seek a cooperative environment with minimum bureaucracy and with quiet time for reflection where they can exercise their imagination.

Interpersonal Style:

These people care deeply for others but are often too busy to spend time with them outside of work. They seldom express their feelings outwardly, but remain loyal and devoted to people and causes. They often communicate their feelings best through writing rather than speaking. They work most effectively alone without interruption.

Possible Developmental Needs:

They may need to develop skills for the realistic and detailed planning of projects. It may be important for them to develop a more tough-minded stance, along with the ability to say no. They may sometimes have to lower their sights to avoid a self-defeating attitude of perfectionism.

[√] I N T P

Inquisitive Analyzer

Profile:

Intensely analytical and objectively critical, these people are hair-splitting logicians. Mainly interested in ideas and intensely curious, they have little liking for small talk or parties. They are quiet and reserved, but can be counted on to discuss in detail any subject they have studied or about which they have thought deeply. They learn quickly, and their insight, ingenuity, and intellectual curiosity are strengthened by their intuitive powers. They have sharply defined interests, are persevering and thorough, and are unimpressed by authority.

Attributes:

Autonomous, cognitive, curious, detached, independent, inquisitive, logical, original, precise, reflective, reserved, self-determined, skeptical, speculative, theoretical.

Preferred Work Environment:

These people thrive in an unstructured environment that fosters independence, offering privacy and the opportunity to work quietly and intently on difficult problems. They value hardworking colleagues who are similarly engrossed in challenging pursuits.

Interpersonal Style:

Quiet and reserved, these people rely heavily on their strong logical ability to relate to others. They enjoy talking about "important" subjects and cannot tolerate small talk. They have difficulty expressing their emotions and are difficult to get to know.

Possible Developmental Needs:

They may need to better understand the needs of others and communicate more clearly, conveying ideas in simpler terms that all can understand. It may be important to spend more time on the practical details and follow-through required in some projects.

[√] ESTP

Realistic Adapter in the World of Material Things

Profile:

These are the matter-of-fact people. They rely on what they see, hear, and perceive directly. They are confident that they will find a solution for any problem once they understand all of the pertinent facts. They work best with tangible things that can be worked, handled, taken apart, or put together. They have a strong and active curiosity about anything they can see, smell, touch, hear, or taste, especially when it is new. Excellent problem-solvers, they recognize the specific need of the moment and meet it. They can absorb, apply, and remember great numbers of facts; display a strong artistic judgment and taste; and handle tools and materials with great skill. They are highly resourceful and make good negotiators.

Attributes:

Activity-oriented, adaptable, alert, charming, easygoing, energetic, friendly, fun-loving, good-natured, observant, outgoing, persuasive, popular, pragmatic, quick, realistic, spontaneous, versatile.

Preferred Work Environment:

These people prefer a flexible, technical environment with a minimum of regulations, time to enjoy themselves while responding to the needs of the moment, and colleagues who value firsthand experience. They prefer to work in an attractive place.

Interpersonal Style:

They are diplomatic negotiators and very aware of what others want and need. ESTPs are amusing, interesting, and fun to be around. They are risk-takers and tend to be adventurous in their relationships.

Possible Developmental Needs:

They may need to temper their spontaneous and sometimes reckless actions with realistic planning and a deeper sense of commitment to a worthwhile project or cause. They may need to channel their high energy toward more constructive goals.

[√] E S F P

Realistic Adapter in Human Relationships

Profile:

Easy, outgoing, friendly, and accepting, these people rely directly on their senses. They look for a satisfying solution to emerge instead of trying to impose one they think should or must be right. They are infectious in their enjoyment of things and make life more fun for those around them. They are unprejudiced, open-minded, and tolerant of almost everyone, including themselves. They work best in situations requiring common sense and practical ability. They are generous and optimistic, like company and excitement, and are actively curious about people, food, activities, or anything new to their senses. They are tactful and sympathetic and display a real interest in people. They learn best through firsthand experience rather than through books and lectures.

Attributes:

Adaptable, cooperative, easygoing, enthusiastic, friendly, outgoing, playful, pleasant, realistic, sociable, sympathetic, tactful, talkative, tolerant, vivacious, witty.

Preferred Work Environment:

These people prize a lively, energetic, and action-oriented workplace. They want to be among others who are easygoing, reality-oriented, adaptable, people-oriented, and harmonious.

Interpersonal Style:

These people are open-minded and genuinely interested in others. They are fun to be with and are witty, playful, and good conversationalists. They are skilled at conflict resolution and can deal effectively with difficult personal situations on the spot. They mix easily with others and are generally well-liked.

Possible Developmental Needs:

They may need to look twice to be certain that they have not overlooked a problem hiding behind another's affability. They may need to develop a better balance between their leisure and work time. When making decisions, it may be important to think things through logically and to adopt a long-range vision curbing a tendency toward impulsiveness.

[√] E N F P

Warmly Enthusiastic Planner of Change

Profile:

Warmly enthusiastic, high-spirited, ingenious, and imaginative, these people are able to do almost anything that interests them. They are quick with a solution to almost any difficulty and are ready to help anyone with a problem. They are enthusiastic innovators, having considerable energy for carrying to fruition projects that are generated by their own imagination and initiative. Their use of feeling judgment adds depth to the insights provided by their intuition. They are gifted observers and enterprisers and are charming and well-liked.

Attributes:

Adaptive, creative, curious, energetic, enthusiastic, expressive, friendly, gentle, imaginative, independent, individualistic, inspirational, inventive, perceptive, restless, spontaneous, sympathetic, understanding, versatile, warm.

Preferred Work Environment:

These people prefer an environment with a minimum of constraints and a maximum of lively, imaginative colleagues working in a colorful, participative atmosphere emphasizing human potential.

Interpersonal Style:

These people actively maintain their relationships, keep their options open, and do everything they can to avoid conflict and disharmony. They usually have a large network of contacts and are skilled at understanding others. They are characterized as gentle, warm, and sympathetic to others and are good at applying new insights to the solution of personal problems.

Possible Developmental Needs:

It may be important for them to develop an ability to manage their time and projects more effectively, avoid moving on to new projects before the old ones are finished, and give more time to studying relevant details. They may need to become better organized, particularly when it comes to prioritizing their work.

[√] E N T P

Inventive, Analytical Planner of Change

Profile:

Characterized by a quick ingenuity, these are people of many talents. They make stimulating company, are alert and outspoken. They are extremely perceptive about the attitudes of other people and utilize this perception to enroll others in supporting their endeavors. They are objective in their approach to projects and to the people in their lives. They enjoy novelty and uncertainty and move easily from one interest to another. They love challenges, and are pragmatic and goal-oriented. They enjoy feeling competent in a variety of areas and appreciate multiple talents in others as well.

Attributes:

Adaptive, analytical, challenging, clever, creative, enterprising, enthusiastic, independent, individualistic, inspirational, inventive, outspoken, questioning, resourceful, strategic, theoretical.

Preferred Work Environment:

These people prefer an environment that encourages risk-taking and autonomy. They like to work among colleagues who are independent and involved in complex problems, in a flexible atmosphere with few bureaucratic constraints.

Interpersonal Style:

Although they tend toward the impersonal side, they can inspire others with their natural enthusiasm. They prefer to understand rather than judge people and deal imaginatively with their relationships. They are often more concerned about people's effect on their work than on how their work may affect others.

Possible Developmental Needs:

They may find it important to apply themselves to better grasping and following through on the details of a project to ensure that the project is neither poorly selected nor left unfinished. They may need to set more realistic priorities, targets, and schedules, and acknowledge the contributions required and supplied by others.

[√] ESTJ

Fact-minded, Practical Organizer

Profile:

These people like to organize projects and make sure that they are completed. They tend to focus on the job that needs to get done rather than on the people who need to do it. They are practical, realistic, and matter-of-fact, with a natural head for business or mechanics. They have little interest in subjects for which they see no practical use. They are characterized as responsible, orderly, loyal, and steadfast. They enjoy being involved in community activities. They are more interested in seeing present realities than future possibilities and use past experience and solid facts to help them solve problems. They like projects where the results of their work are immediate, visible, and tangible.

Attributes:

Aggressive, analytic, conscientious, decisive, direct, efficient, fact-minded, forceful, impersonal, logical, objective, organized, practical, responsible, serious, structured, systematic, thorough.

Preferred Work Environment:

These people prefer a hardworking, results-oriented, and structured environment among coworkers who are intensely focused on "getting the job done." They prefer structure and rewards for meeting goals.

Interpersonal Style:

These people are serious, forceful, and thorough and are less concerned with their emotional life than with practical considerations. They maintain consistency in their relationships, can be tough when they need to discipline others, and are easy to get to know and understand—little is hidden. They like to organize and run things.

Possible Developmental Needs:

It may be important for them to develop patience, a slower pace when dealing with others, and a more thoughtful consideration of all the facts as well as the human side of a given situation or project before reaching conclusions. They may need to make a special effort to acknowledge the contribution of others.

[√] ESFJ

Practical Harmonizer and Worker with People

Profile:

Born cooperators, ESFJs are warm-hearted, talkative, popular, and conscientious, and make active committee members. They have a special gift for finding value in other people's opinions. They work best with encouragement and praise and are always doing something nice for someone. They are practical, realistic, and down-to-earth and enjoy their possessions. They are responsible, attentive, loyal, hardworking, and traditional. They derive much of their pleasure and satisfaction from the warmth and appreciation of those around them. These people take little interest in abstract thinking or technical subjects. They are mainly concerned with things that directly and visibly affect people's lives.

Attributes:

Compassionate, conscientious, cooperative, friendly, harmonious, loyal, opinionated, orderly, outgoing, personable, popular, realistic, responsible, responsive, sociable, sympathetic, tactful, thorough, traditional.

Preferred Work Environment:

These people prefer a friendly, cooperative environment that is well-organized and oriented toward achieving defined goals. They like to work with people who are sensitive, friendly, focused on helping others, and appreciative when they are served.

Interpersonal Style:

These people are popular and cooperative. They consider their relationships important and maintain them with energy and intelligence. They are open to the opinions of others but at the same time have their own strong opinions, and are frequently sensitive to indifference or criticism.

Possible Developmental Needs:

It may be important for them to appreciate the value of a detailed and complex analysis of a problem when appropriate. They may need to recognize the value of conflict and accept it when it occurs. Similarly, they may have to open their eyes to the facts in disagreeable or discordant situations.

Imaginative Harmonizer and Worker with People

Profile:

These people generally feel real concern for what others think or want and try to handle things with due regard for other people's feelings. They can present a proposal or lead a group discussion with ease and tact. ENFJs tend to focus on the best qualities in others and are loyal to those they respect, to institutions, and to causes. Sometimes they admire things to the point of idealization. They think best while they are talking to people and are likely to be gifted in their speaking expression and less so in their writing. Natural leaders, they are social, popular, and active, but put considerable time into getting their jobs done. They can be characterized as tolerant, trustworthy, and forgiving.

Attributes:

Caring, concerned, congenial, conscientious, curious, diplomatic, energetic, enthusiastic, expressive, idealistic, loyal, nurturing, opinioned, orderly, personable, popular, responsible, sociable, supportive, verbal.

Preferred Work Environment:

These people prefer an orderly environment with little change and maximum opportunity for self-expression. They value a supportive workplace among colleagues who operate with a spirit of harmony and are dedicated to changing the world for the benefit of humanity.

Interpersonal Style:

These people are nurturing and supportive and show an unusual amount of regard for others. They are popular and make good public speakers. They openly express their concern and responsibility for others and are seldom critical. They are usually gracious and socially adept.

Possible Developmental Needs:

They may need to develop an ability to manage conflict in a productive way. It may be important to set aside personal feelings and relationships when the facts warrant an objective look at a situation. They may need to recognize people's limitations and learn that blind loyalty can be a detriment.

[√] ENTJ

Intuitive, Innovative Organizer

Profile:

These people enjoy executive action and run as much of the world as they can get their hands on. They like to think ahead, organize plans, and make a systematic effort to reach their objectives on schedule. They seek leadership roles and express themselves in a hearty and frank way. They are able in their studies and work. They are usually well-informed and enjoy adding to their fund of knowledge. They are seldom content in jobs that make no demand on their intuition. They have a strong desire to give structure to projects. They strive for efficiency and effectiveness and can be tough when the situation calls for it.

Attributes:

Aggressive, analytical, challenging, controlled, critical, decisive, fair, innovative, intuitive, logical, objective, organized, straightforward, strategic, systematic, theoretical, tough.

Preferred Work Environment:

These people want to work among tough-minded and independent colleagues in a structured but challenging, goal-oriented environment that rewards firm decision-making.

Interpersonal Style:

These people have a strong need to lead others and drive them as hard as they drive themselves. They value logic and have little patience with confusion and inefficiency. They are critical and can be insensitive to the feelings of others.

Possible Developmental Needs:

They may need to develop greater sensitivity and learn to acknowledge the contributions of others when the situation demands it. It may be important for them to be more thorough in developing a plan and understanding the facts in detail before making decisions. Similarly, they should perhaps avoid communicating confidence before the situation actually justifies it. They may benefit greatly by bringing more sensing types into their immediate environment.

Summarizing Your Own Work Type and Style

When you have completed reading about your style, use your own words to summarize the material that describes it. Copy only those portions of the description that you feel apply to you. Add any additional ideas, thoughts, or feelings that you have about your style. Write as much as you feel necessary to describe yourself fully and with satisfaction. See pages 92–105 in Chapter 8 for examples of such a description.

Summary:

If you would like to learn more about your type, we suggest you take the MBTI®. The MBTI® is a well-researched and validated instrument that only trained, qualified individuals are allowed to purchase and administer. In order to find out where you can take the MBTI® and have it interpreted, you may want to contact the following organizations, which promote the understanding and ethical use of psychological-type theory and will be able to provide you with MBTI® resources in your area: Association for Psychological Type (APT), P.O. Box 5099, Gainesville, FL 32609, (904) 371-1853; Center for Applications of Psychological Type (CAPT), 2720 NW Sixth Street, Gainesville, FL 32609, (940) 375-1060; Consulting Psychologists Press, 577 College Avenue, Palo Alto, CA 94306-1490, (415) 857-1444.

4

CAREER TYPE

In addition to your work type, there is a way of describing your natural career preferences—your career type.

Career type has to do with the relationship of your personality to the kinds of work you like to do, the occupations you choose, and the work environment in which you thrive.

Several career specialists have made direct connections between personality traits and career orientations. The most notable of these researchers, John Holland, introduced six personality/occupation types that we call here career types:

1. (R) Realistic
2. (I) Investigative
3. (A) Artistic
4. (S) Social
5. (E) Enterprising
6. (C) Conventional

Assessing Your Career Type

While there are various assessment instruments that can be administered to indicate career type, it is both informative and interesting to determine your own career type by self-assessment. The process is simple.

On the following pages, each of the six career types is described in detail. You will read through each of the six types and select the one you consider to provide the most accurate description of your own career type or style. In addition, you will select second and third career types that you feel address some aspect of your own career type or style.

Realistic

Profile:

Typically, these are people who prefer to deal more with things than with people or ideas, are more oriented to the present than to the past or future, and have highly structured patterns of thought. They perceive themselves as having mechanical and athletic ability. They are apt to value tangible things or personal characteristics that lend themselves to easy evaluation—money, power, and status. They generally avoid goals, values, and tasks that require a subjective or intellectual approach or social skills. Realistic people prefer actions to words and are impatient with those who would rather talk about issues than do something about them. They take pride in producing useful things that are well made. They tend to be conservative in their attitudes and values, which are based on premises they have tested and found reliable, "tried and true." Individuals of this type can be found in engineering, skilled trades, agriculture, and technical vocations.

Attributes:

Aggressive, concrete, conservative, frank, hands-on, independent, persistent, physical, practical, rugged individualist, self-reliant, stable, strong, thrifty, traditional, well-coordinated.

Preferred Work Environment:

Realistic types prefer outdoor work or working in laboratories, factories, or machine shops with their hands, where they can wear casual clothes and be with familiar people. They like working in teams where the achievement of making something useful or completing a physical task is valued. They prefer structured work environments.

Interpersonal Style:

They usually have a small group of very close friends with whom they spend most of their time and maintain these friendships over long periods. They may be wary of outsiders who come into their environment who dress, look, or speak differently. They can be extremely loyal to people, organizations, and causes or ideals that have traditional appeal.

Possible Developmental Needs:

It may be important for realistic types to develop stronger interpersonal communication skills. They may need to learn to acknowledge the qualities and/or needs of others, be more active in seeking relationships with people who are different from them, and be more open to new ideas.

Typical Occupations and Job Titles:

Architect, athletic trainer, bus driver, carpenter, electrician, emergency medical technician, engineer, farmer, forester, horticulturist, military officer, physical education teacher, police officer, radiology technician, veterinarian, vocational teacher.

Investigative

Profile:

These individuals are characterized as analytical and comfortable with abstractions, and prefer to cope with life and its problems by applying their formidable analytical skills. They are often scholarly and self-confident, and have mathematical and scientific ability. They may hold conservative attitudes and values, often handle interpersonal and group relationships with difficulty, and achieve primarily in the academic and scientific fields. They are likely to possess a high degree of originality, as well as verbal and mathematical skills. Individuals with this orientation tend to be found in occupations related to science, math, social science, and other technical areas, including computer science, engineering, and the medical sciences.

Attributes:

Analytical, creative, curious, explorative, independent, inquisitive, intellectual, original, precise, rational, unconventional.

Preferred Work Environment:

Investigative types prefer to work in laboratories, libraries, universities, or other places where their inquisitive nature and interest in research and investigation is well supported. They tend to work best as individual contributors, although they can be effective team members when properly motivated and when allowed to perform independent tasks at appropriate times. They prefer to work with others who are achievement-oriented and who prize intelligence and logical thinking.

Interpersonal Style:

They usually prefer a strong, even argumentative, intellectual discussion about a topic of particular interest in their field of expertise to any other kind of interaction. Investigative types may appear withdrawn when they are deeply involved in a project or learning a new skill or concept. They can have faithful and long-term relationships, usually with a small number of close friends or colleagues. They gravitate toward people who share their lifestyle and intellectual interests.

Possible Developmental Needs:

They may need to develop stronger interpersonal skills, especially if they are involved in management. Assertiveness and leadership training, along with developing the ability to communicate abstract ideas, clearly may be helpful. Some investigative types may also need training in organizing their work more efficiently and in making decisions in a more timely and practical way.

Typical Occupations and Job Titles:

Biologist, chemist, chiropractor, college professor, computer programmer, dentist, dietitian, geographer, geologist, mathematician, medical technician, nurse, optometrist, pharmacist, physical therapist, physician, physicist, psychologist, research and development manager, science teacher, sociologist, systems analyst, veterinarian.

Artistic

Profile:

These are people who like to express their innermost feelings and imagination in their work. They are expressive, original, intuitive, nonconforming, introspective, and independent, and have artistic and musical ability (acting, writing, painting, sculpting, etc.). Their most important way of communicating is through their art. Artistic types pursue occupations related to music, literature, the fine arts, the dramatic arts, advertising, journalism, or a wide range of design fields, including the design of programs and services, and countless other creative forms.

Attributes:

Creative, emotional, expressive, idealistic, imaginative, impulsive, independent, intuitive, nonconforming, original, spontaneous.

Preferred Work Environment:

Artistic people prefer unstructured, informal, private places where they can work alone or with a group of people involved in a single project where they have considerable latitude for self-expression. The often work best unsupervised in an environment where quality is more valued than quantity.

Interpersonal Style:

While they prefer to use the product of their work to express their feelings and thoughts, they are able to communicate with style and flair and express their ideas with emotion and strength. Artistic types prefer to be with people who are similarly involved in activities requiring creative expression and the fashioning of artistic products.

Possible Developmental Needs:

It may be important for them to develop communication skills that use logic and organization. They may need to develop planning skills and practice working with others in an environment requiring cooperation. They may need to give more attention to caring about and respecting the ideas of others. They may also need to give more attention to details and gather more factual information.

Typical Occupations and Job Titles:

Actor, actress, advertising copywriter, architect, art teacher, author, ballet dancer, beautician, broadcaster, chef, cinematographer, commercial artist, film director, fine artist, illustrator, interior decorator, journalist, linguist, medical illustrator, musician, photographer, playwright, sculptor.

Social

Profile:

Persons with a social orientation are deeply interested in other people, are sensitive to their needs, and concerned for their welfare. They like to help others, understand others, have teaching abilities, and often lack mechanical and scientific aptitude. They value social activities, solving social problems, and interpersonal relations. They utilize their verbal and social skills to influence other people's behavior. They usually are cheerful, impulsive, scholarly, and verbally oriented. Individuals with this orientation tend to be in teaching, health care, social welfare positions, service-oriented industries and professions, and the helping vocations.

Attributes:

Concerned, cooperative, ethical, friendly, generous, genuine, helpful, humanistic, kind, perceptive, responsible, sensitive, sociable, supportive, tactful, understanding.

Preferred Work Environment:

Social types work well in a wide variety of environments. They prefer to work with others in the immediate service of people or in forwarding ideas and activities that contribute to the improvement of society at large. They are good team players and prefer a congenial, harmonious environment in which to pursue aims targeted at specific achievement.

Interpersonal Style:

These people are characterized as warm, friendly, open, and communicative. They may have a wide circle of friends and colleagues with whom they share a deep appreciation of the quality and value of diversity in people. They understand the feelings of others and may often serve as informal counselors to their friends.

Possible Developmental Needs:

Social types may need to develop more effective management and organizational skills, including team building and leadership. It may be important for them to develop an appreciation for financial planning and the constraints involved in budgeting, as well as the importance of administrative efficiency and organization. They may also need to develop assertiveness and conflict-management skills and pay more attention to political realities.

Typical Occupations and Job Titles:

Concierge, consumer advocate, environmental attorney, human resources generalist, guidance counselor, legal aid attorney, minister, nurse, occupational therapist, physician, psychologist, social worker, teacher, training and development specialist, travel agent.

Enterprising

Profile:

Enterprising people tend to be adventurous, dominant, and persuasive. They place high value on political and economic matters and are drawn to power and leadership roles. They perceive themselves as aggressive, popular, self-confident, social, possessing leadership and speaking abilities, and lacking scientific ability. They thrive on influencing others and employ their considerable social skills to obtain political ends or achieve economic goals. Individuals with this orientation tend to be found in occupations related to sales, marketing, and management, or in the professions of law, politics, and consulting.

Attributes:

Adventuresome, aggressive, ambitious, assertive, competitive, confident, domineering, energetic, persuasive, political, sociable, status-conscious, verbal.

Preferred Work Environment:

Enterprising individuals prefer to work in a hard-driving, well-organized, results-oriented environment where people are dedicated to achieving bottom-line results. They are leaders who are adept at organizing others to produce a well-defined and valuable product or service for which they receive a high compensation.

Interpersonal Style:

Outgoing, strong communicators, enterprising people work hard at getting along with others, particularly when it is important for them to achieve results. They may have a wide network of professional and personal contacts with whom they stay in active communication. They are highly energetic and may use their skills and other personal assets to benefit their community and society at large.

Possible Developmental Needs:

They may need to develop greater empathy and learn to respect the ideas of others. It may be important to enhance their team-building skills—by improving personal communication, acknowledging others, and stating expectations clearly—to achieve the best results.

Typical Occupations and Job Titles:

Attorney, business executive, business manager, chef/owner, entrepreneur, florist, funeral director, life insurance agent, optician, political activist, public official, purchasing agent, realtor, restaurant manager, retail buyer, salesperson, store manager, travel agent/owner.

Conventional

Profile:

Conventional individuals tend to be precise and organized, and work well in structured situations. They feel most comfortable with precise language and frequently exhibit accurate accounting abilities. They are often conservative and orderly, with administrative and information- and data-collection skills. They value business and economic achievement, material possessions, and status. Individuals with this orientation tend to be found in financial services, business, computations, administration, office practice systems, and staff support advisory roles.

Attributes:

Accurate, careful, conforming, conscientious, conservative, efficient, orderly, organized, persevering, persistent, practical, precise, predictable, quiet, responsible, systematic.

Preferred Work Environment:

Conventional people prefer the structured, orderly environment of the office of an organized company with clear and well-defined rules and policies. They work well on teams when they have a clearly defined task that they can accomplish on their own and contribute back to the overall success of the team. They are loyal and hardworking subordinates when they are working for a leader who appreciates their contribution. As managers they value efficiency and work best in a structured, goal-oriented fashion. They value security and dislike ambiguous, fast-changing environments.

Interpersonal Style:

Often reserved, conventional people rely on their work to communicate for them. They form relationships slowly, resist change, and are likely to have a small group of long-term close friends with whom they share common experiences and lifestyle preferences.

Possible Developmental Needs:

They may need to develop more skill at expanding their methods of problem-solving. It may also be important for them to learn techniques for handling change, making decisions under conditions of uncertainty, and being more assertive.

Typical Occupations and Job Titles:

Accountant, banker, business teacher, credit manager, dental assistant, dietitian, food service manager, housekeeping manager, IRS agent, math teacher, military enlisted personnel, nursing home administrator, office manager, secretary.

Summarizing Your Results

After you have determined your three top career types, write them in the spaces below. Repeat the first letter of each type in the parentheses. This three-letter set constitutes your Holland code and expresses your overall occupational orientation. Note that some jobs appear in more than one career type (for example, architecture attracts both realistic and artistic types and nursing attracts both investigative and social types).

Primary Career Type: (   ) _____

Secondary Career Type: (   ) _____

Tertiary Career Type: (   ) _____

Now use your own words to synthesize and summarize the material that describes your primary, secondary, and tertiary career types. Copy only those portions that you feel apply directly to you. Add any additional ideas, thoughts, or feelings that you have about your types. Write as much as you feel necessary to describe yourself fully and with satisfaction. See pages 92–105 in Chapter 8 for examples of such a description.

Summary:

[√] ASSESSING YOUR CAREER INTERESTS

At the end of the first paragraph of the career types described in this chapter, the typical occupations toward which the career type tends to gravitate are discussed in broad terms. In the last paragraph is a list of the typical occupations and job titles associated with that career type. Read through these lists for your primary, secondary, and tertiary career type and write down any occupations or job titles that are of interest to you. Add any occupational groups or job titles that appeal to you that may not be included on the lists.

Priority   *Career Interests*

[   ] _____

[   ] _____

[   ] _____

[   ] _____

[   ] _____

[   ] _____

[   ] _____

[   ] _____

[   ] _____

[   ] _____

[   ] _____

[   ] _____

[   ] _____

[   ] _____

[   ] _____

Write a 1 in the space to the left of the occupation or job title you consider to be the one of greatest interest to you, a 2 for the next most important, etc., until you have selected the five occupations or job titles of greatest interest to you.

5

SKILLS

Skills are those specific talents, abilities and personal qualities that enable people to accomplish things and make a contribution to the world. Many people are not entirely aware of the full range of skills they possess. Their perception of what constitutes a skill may be limited to certain technical procedures learned in school or through training. Many simply identify themselves with their job title and recognize only skills they utilize in getting their immediate jobs done.

With the following assessment, you'll discover the broad spectrum of skills with which you function in the world and recognize those that are most important to your satisfaction, well-being, and success.

What Is a Skill?

The dictionary defines skill as "great ability or proficiency; expertness; an art, craft, or science, especially one involving the use of the hands or body; ability in such an art, craft, or science."

When you work, your skills are what you use to get things done, to accomplish your goals, to achieve your purposes. (Remember that all skills can be *improved* with practice and development. There are many resources available to help you do this. See Chapter 9 for further references.) For our purposes, skills can be classified in three major categories: functional, adaptive, and specific content. Each is described below.

Functional People, Data, and Physical Skills

Wherever and however you work, you are always interacting and dealing with some combination of people, information, and objects. Your *functional skills* are the ones you use to organize information logically, communicate clearly, write with style, lift heavy objects, analyze and solve problems, make decisions, and relate effectively to people.

54

People skills apply specifically to interpersonal communication of all sorts—supervision, management, counseling, motivation, entertainment, teaching, serving, negotiating, persuading—in short, every form of relating to others.

Data skills comprise every form of collecting, handling, and dispensing information. The information may appear in any qualifiable or quantifiable format: facts, figures, even ideas or emotions. Broadly speaking, whatever cannot be classified as a person or an object may qualify in some way or other as data. Data activities include any form of analyzing, interpreting, and judging, and the sending and receiving of information of any kind.

Physical skills have to do with the physical manipulation of real objects. Repairing, lifting, moving, making, typing, building, carrying, sawing, cutting, carving, filing, driving, handling, and holding are activities requiring physical skills. Dancing, walking, running, and activities requiring dexterity, physical strength, coordination, prowess, or rhythm are similarly categorized.

Most of the activities you engage in, and hence the skills you have, relate to all three categories. For example, when you write a letter on a word processor or typewriter or by hand describing some fact or situation, you're combining a people activity (communicating), a physical activity (typing or writing), and a data activity (conveying information).

Note whether you consider yourself to be primarily a "people person," a "data person," or a "physical person," and which of the other two is secondary and which is tertiary.

Adaptive Skills

Adaptive skills (sometimes called self-management skills or personal qualities and characteristics) are those behavior- or temperament-based qualities developed while growing up, which you first cultivated in order to fit into (or adapt to) a variety of environments, starting with your home, school, and friends, and which you now bring into the world of work. Many personality traits and characteristics qualify as skills or aptitudes because they enable you to accomplish things. Persistence, confidence, thoroughness, patience, sensitivity, assertiveness, time management, and flexibility are certainly qualities that improve work effectiveness. Often, your overall personality may be your greatest asset. Poor adaptive skills, on the other hand, are a serious drawback, and constitute the reason most frequently cited by employers for firing someone.

Specific Content Skills

Specific content skills are knowledge-based and the ones used only in a particular job with little or no transferability to other kinds of work. Examples include knowing how to operate a specific mainframe computer, operate a tower crane, perform open-heart surgery, assemble microcircuit boards, interpret tax law, make out a tax return, use a specific computer language, or grow orchids.

The beauty of adaptive and functional skills, by contrast, is that they are transferable. You can take them with you from one job or career to almost any other.

Motivated Skills

The most important group of skills for you to recognize and evaluate comprises those functional, adaptive, and specific content skills that you are particularly *motivated* to include and utilize in your worklife. The motivation comes from the enjoyment and effectiveness of using those skills. The more you use them, the greater your worklife satisfaction.

Read through the following skill lists, and for those you most prefer to use in your worklife (your motivated skills), check whether your current level of ability in that skill is acceptable or needs development.

By "acceptable" we mean that you consider yourself to be *reasonably effective* in utilizing a given skill. Give yourself the benefit of the doubt and make sure not to think in terms of all or nothing, or make excessive, perfectionistic demands on yourself as you rate your skills.

By "needs development," we refer to those skills at which you consider yourself to be *less than reasonably effective* and that you need to improve in order to enhance your effectiveness at work. Space is also provided for you to add skills that may not be included on these lists.

Although specific content skills are no less important than functional and adaptive skills, they are not included in the inventories that follow. Most people are far more aware of these skills than they are of the broader or more generic skill areas.

When you read through the skills, think, "I like to or would like to . . . ," and complete the sentence with the appropriate skills from the lists.

[√] FUNCTIONAL PEOPLE SKILLS

Remember, check only those skills that you are motivated to use in your worklife.

"I like to or would like to . . ."

Acceptable
Needs Development

[ ] [ ] Acknowledge others
[ ] [ ] Act as liaison
[ ] [ ] Act as mentor
[ ] [ ] Act assertively
[ ] [ ] Appraise and develop others
[ ] [ ] Assist others to make decisions and solve problems
[ ] [ ] Build teams
[ ] [ ] Coach
[ ] [ ] Communicate clearly
[ ] [ ] Communicate effectively
[ ] [ ] Consult
[ ] [ ] Coordinate people for effective performance
[ ] [ ] Counsel and advise people
[ ] [ ] Criticize constructively
[ ] [ ] Delegate
[ ] [ ] Develop good relationships
[ ] [ ] Develop potential in others
[ ] [ ] Develop rapport with others
[ ] [ ] Entertain
[ ] [ ] Evaluate performance of others
[ ] [ ] Express feelings
[ ] [ ] Express ideas
[ ] [ ] Facilitate groups
[ ] [ ] Follow instructions
[ ] [ ] Have empathy
[ ] [ ] Heal people
[ ] [ ] Help others
[ ] [ ] Identify people's problems
[ ] [ ] Influence others
[ ] [ ] Interview others
[ ] [ ] Keep groups on track and moving
[ ] [ ] Lead others
[ ] [ ] Listen attentively

Acceptable
Needs Development

[ ] [ ] Listen with empathy
[ ] [ ] Manage conflict
[ ] [ ] Manage people
[ ] [ ] Mediate
[ ] [ ] Motivate others
[ ] [ ] Negotiate contracts and agreements
[ ] [ ] Negotiate prices
[ ] [ ] Network
[ ] [ ] Persuade others
[ ] [ ] Plan social occasions and activities
[ ] [ ] Promote ideas
[ ] [ ] Provide others with information
[ ] [ ] Relate to a wide variety of people
[ ] [ ] Resolve conflict
[ ] [ ] Select people for positions
[ ] [ ] Sell products
[ ] [ ] Sell services
[ ] [ ] Serve customers
[ ] [ ] Serve others
[ ] [ ] Settle disputes
[ ] [ ] Show warmth and support
[ ] [ ] Speak well in public
[ ] [ ] Supervise
[ ] [ ] Teach
[ ] [ ] Train people
[ ] [ ] Tune in to needs and feelings of others
[ ] [ ] Understand behavior
[ ] [ ] Work effectively on a team
[ ] [ ] _____
[ ] [ ] _____
[ ] [ ] _____
[ ] [ ] _____
[ ] [ ] _____

[✓] FUNCTIONAL DATA SKILLS

Remember, check only those skills that you are motivated to use in your worklife.

"I like to or would like to . . ."

Acceptable	Needs Development		
[ ]	[ ]	Administer policies and programs
[ ]	[ ]	Allocate resources
[ ]	[ ]	Analyze facts and ideas
[ ]	[ ]	Analyze financial data
[ ]	[ ]	Analyze needs
[ ]	[ ]	Analyze plans
[ ]	[ ]	Anticipate problems
[ ]	[ ]	Arrange events
[ ]	[ ]	Assess art
[ ]	[ ]	Attend to details
[ ]	[ ]	Brainstorm
[ ]	[ ]	Calculate risks
[ ]	[ ]	Champion a cause
[ ]	[ ]	Classify things and ideas
[ ]	[ ]	Compute
[ ]	[ ]	Conceive, create, and develop ideas
[ ]	[ ]	Conceptualize
[ ]	[ ]	Control inventory
[ ]	[ ]	Coordinate events and operations
[ ]	[ ]	Critique performance
[ ]	[ ]	Critique writing
[ ]	[ ]	Delegate responsibility
[ ]	[ ]	Design architecture
[ ]	[ ]	Design and develop systems
[ ]	[ ]	Design interiors
[ ]	[ ]	Design training programs
[ ]	[ ]	Determine policy
[ ]	[ ]	Develop structure
[ ]	[ ]	Diagnose problems
[ ]	[ ]	Do pricing
[ ]	[ ]	Edit and proofread
[ ]	[ ]	Establish procedures
[ ]	[ ]	Estimate costs
[ ]	[ ]	Estimate material quantities

Acceptable	Needs Development		
[ ]	[ ]	Evaluate data and ideas
[ ]	[ ]	Expedite
[ ]	[ ]	Follow instructions
[ ]	[ ]	Forecast trends
[ ]	[ ]	Gather information and data
[ ]	[ ]	Implement/follow through
[ ]	[ ]	Improvise
[ ]	[ ]	Initiate and promote change
[ ]	[ ]	Innovate
[ ]	[ ]	Interview for information
[ ]	[ ]	Invent
[ ]	[ ]	Inventory
[ ]	[ ]	Investigate
[ ]	[ ]	Keep financial books
[ ]	[ ]	Keep records
[ ]	[ ]	Maintain schedules
[ ]	[ ]	Make decisions
[ ]	[ ]	Manage budgets
[ ]	[ ]	Manage logistics
[ ]	[ ]	Manage projects
[ ]	[ ]	Match people to tasks
[ ]	[ ]	Monitor and regulate work flow
[ ]	[ ]	Navigate a course
[ ]	[ ]	Observe details
[ ]	[ ]	Operate a computer terminal
[ ]	[ ]	Organize information logically
[ ]	[ ]	Organize people
[ ]	[ ]	Organize projects
[ ]	[ ]	Perceive and define cause-and-effect relationships
[ ]	[ ]	Plan projects
[ ]	[ ]	Plan strategically
[ ]	[ ]	Plan work assignments
[ ]	[ ]	Prepare budgets
[ ]	[ ]	Prepare financial data

[ ] [ ] Present information logically
[ ] [ ] Produce events
[ ] [ ] Provide organizational
    structure
[ ] [ ] Purchase materials
[ ] [ ] Read technical information
[ ] [ ] Research subjects
[ ] [ ] Solve math problems
[ ] [ ] Solve problems
[ ] [ ] Solve statistical problems
[ ] [ ] Synthesize facts and ideas
[ ] [ ] Systematize materials and
    operations
[ ] [ ] Think logically
[ ] [ ] Troubleshoot and correct
    problems
[ ] [ ] Understand complex
    material
[ ] [ ] Understand finances
[ ] [ ] Use intuition
[ ] [ ] Use mathematics
[ ] [ ] Use statistics
[ ] [ ] Work with abstract material/
    concepts
[ ] [ ] Work with blueprints
[ ] [ ] Work within structure
[ ] [ ] Write creatively
[ ] [ ] Write promotion and
    publicity
[ ] [ ] Write proposals
[ ] [ ] Write technical material
[ ] [ ] _____
[ ] [ ] _____
[ ] [ ] _____
[ ] [ ] _____
[ ] [ ] _____
[ ] [ ] _____
[ ] [ ] _____
[ ] [ ] _____
[ ] [ ] _____
[ ] [ ] _____

[ ] [ ] _____
[ ] [ ] _____
[ ] [ ] _____
[ ] [ ] _____
[ ] [ ] _____
[ ] [ ] _____
[ ] [ ] _____
[ ] [ ] _____
[ ] [ ] _____
[ ] [ ] _____
[ ] [ ] _____
[ ] [ ] _____
[ ] [ ] _____
[ ] [ ] _____
[ ] [ ] _____
[ ] [ ] _____
[ ] [ ] _____
[ ] [ ] _____
[ ] [ ] _____
[ ] [ ] _____
[ ] [ ] _____
[ ] [ ] _____
[ ] [ ] _____
[ ] [ ] _____
[ ] [ ] _____
[ ] [ ] _____
[ ] [ ] _____
[ ] [ ] _____
[ ] [ ] _____
[ ] [ ] _____
[ ] [ ] _____

[√] FUNCTIONAL PHYSICAL SKILLS

Remember, check only those skills that you are motivated to use in your worklife.

"I like to or would like to . . ."

Acceptable	Needs Development	
[ ]	[ ]	Act
[ ]	[ ]	Assemble things
[ ]	[ ]	Be athletic
[ ]	[ ]	Build with wood
[ ]	[ ]	Clean thoroughly
[ ]	[ ]	Construct things
[ ]	[ ]	Cook
[ ]	[ ]	Dance
[ ]	[ ]	Design furniture
[ ]	[ ]	Diagnose mechanical problems
[ ]	[ ]	Display things
[ ]	[ ]	Do body work
[ ]	[ ]	Do carpentry
[ ]	[ ]	Do craft work
[ ]	[ ]	Do electrical work
[ ]	[ ]	Do farming
[ ]	[ ]	Do ironwork
[ ]	[ ]	Do masonry
[ ]	[ ]	Do plumbing
[ ]	[ ]	Do precision work
[ ]	[ ]	Do sheet-metal work
[ ]	[ ]	Drafting
[ ]	[ ]	Draw illustrations
[ ]	[ ]	Drive heavy equipment
[ ]	[ ]	Drive vehicles
[ ]	[ ]	Garden
[ ]	[ ]	Grow things
[ ]	[ ]	Have good spatial perception
[ ]	[ ]	Inspect construction
[ ]	[ ]	Lay bricks
[ ]	[ ]	Maintain equipment
[ ]	[ ]	Maintain physical stamina
[ ]	[ ]	Move with good physical coordination
[ ]	[ ]	Operate heavy machinery
[ ]	[ ]	Operate office equipment

Acceptable	Needs Development	
[ ]	[ ]	Paint
[ ]	[ ]	Perform
[ ]	[ ]	Play a musical instrument
[ ]	[ ]	Repair things
[ ]	[ ]	Sculpt
[ ]	[ ]	Sing
[ ]	[ ]	Sort
[ ]	[ ]	Survey
[ ]	[ ]	Survive in the wilderness
[ ]	[ ]	Take care of living things
[ ]	[ ]	Take quality photographs
[ ]	[ ]	Type
[ ]	[ ]	Use finger dexterity
[ ]	[ ]	Use hand tools
[ ]	[ ]	Use manual dexterity
[ ]	[ ]	Use physical strength
[ ]	[ ]	Use power tools
[ ]	[ ]	Use weapons
[ ]	[ ]	Visualize size and shape
[ ]	[ ]	Work outdoors
[ ]	[ ]	Work with animals
[ ]	[ ]	Work with instruments
[ ]	[ ]	Work with machines
[ ]	[ ]	Work with nature
[ ]	[ ]	_____
[ ]	[ ]	_____
[ ]	[ ]	_____
[ ]	[ ]	_____
[ ]	[ ]	_____
[ ]	[ ]	_____
[ ]	[ ]	_____
[ ]	[ ]	_____
[ ]	[ ]	_____
[ ]	[ ]	_____

[√] MOST IMPORTANT FUNCTIONAL SKILLS CURRENTLY AT AN ACCEPTABLE LEVEL OF DEVELOPMENT

From the lists that you just checked, select up to five people skills, five data skills, and five physical skills that you would most like to include in your worklife and that are currently at an acceptable level of development. You need not include all three categories if you wish to concentrate on only one or two. Write them in order of enjoyment. You can include more than one skill on a line if you feel they are related and form a skill cluster.

PEOPLE SKILLS:

1. _____
2. _____
3. _____
4. _____
5. _____

DATA SKILLS:

1. _____
2. _____
3. _____
4. _____
5. _____

PHYSICAL SKILLS:

1. _____
2. _____
3. _____
4. _____
5. _____

[√] MOST IMPORTANT FUNCTIONAL SKILLS CURRENTLY IN NEED OF DEVELOPMENT

From the lists that you just checked, select up to five people skills, five data skills, and five physical skills that you would most like to include in your worklife and that you checked as needing development. You need not include all three categories if you wish to concentrate on only one or two. Write them in order of your perceived need for development. You can include more than one skill on a line if you feel they are related and form a skill cluster.

PEOPLE SKILLS:

1. _____
2. _____
3. _____
4. _____
5. _____

DATA SKILLS:

1. _____
2. _____
3. _____
4. _____
5. _____

PHYSICAL SKILLS:

1. _____
2. _____
3. _____
4. _____
5. _____

Assessing Your Adaptive Skills (Positive Personal Qualities and Characteristics)

Recognition of your positive personal qualities and characteristics is critically important in building self-esteem. The expression of these characteristics plays a key role in work effectiveness, performance, and job satisfaction.

Therefore, we have included an extensive list of these adaptive skills. The list has been developed with some redundancy or overlap, since there are different ways of describing and perceiving qualities, some of which are rather subtle. It's all right for there to be some duplication in your checked list of characteristics. The most important part of the exercise is recognizing and acknowledging your own best qualities.

It is particularly informative to compare your adaptive skills with the information you discovered about yourself in the previous chapters on style and career type. These comparisons will help you to focus on what is really true for you and will serve to support you in writing a more comprehensive and accurate Personal Career Profile.

Read through the following lists, and for those adaptive skills that are most important to you in your worklife, check whether the level at which you currently express or exercise that quality is acceptable or needs development. Again, do not be overly judgmental or perfectionistic, or think in all-or-nothing terms. Space is also provided for you to add qualities that may not be included on these lists. When you read through the qualities, think, "I am [or have] or would like to be [or to have]. . . ," and complete the sentence with the appropriate qualities from the lists.

[√] ADAPTIVE SKILLS/PERSONAL QUALITIES

Remember, check only those qualities that you are motivated to use in your worklife.

"I am [or have] or would like to be [or to have] . . ."

Acceptable	Needs Development	
[ ]	[ ]	A balanced life
[ ]	[ ]	A good judge of others
[ ]	[ ]	A good listener
[ ]	[ ]	A good sense of self
[ ]	[ ]	A good team player
[ ]	[ ]	A problem-solver
[ ]	[ ]	A quick learner
[ ]	[ ]	A risk-taker
[ ]	[ ]	A sense of humor
[ ]	[ ]	A strong sense of conviction
[ ]	[ ]	Able to admit mistakes
[ ]	[ ]	Able to "deliver" on time
[ ]	[ ]	Able to express feelings in an open and direct manner
[ ]	[ ]	Able to express ideas freely
[ ]	[ ]	Able to follow through
[ ]	[ ]	Able to get along well with others
[ ]	[ ]	Able to get to the heart of problems
[ ]	[ ]	Able to keep my temper in the face of provocation
[ ]	[ ]	Able to plan effectively
[ ]	[ ]	Able to set priorities well
[ ]	[ ]	Able to take criticism
[ ]	[ ]	Able to think things out before acting
[ ]	[ ]	Able to think quickly on my feet
[ ]	[ ]	Able to use time effectively
[ ]	[ ]	Able to work well in a structured environment
[ ]	[ ]	Able to work well under stress
[ ]	[ ]	Academic
[ ]	[ ]	Accepting
[ ]	[ ]	Accurate

Acceptable	Needs Development	
[ ]	[ ]	Achievement-oriented
[ ]	[ ]	Action-oriented
[ ]	[ ]	Active
[ ]	[ ]	Adaptable to change
[ ]	[ ]	Adventurous
[ ]	[ ]	Aggressive
[ ]	[ ]	Alert
[ ]	[ ]	Ambitious
[ ]	[ ]	Analytical
[ ]	[ ]	Assertive
[ ]	[ ]	Astute
[ ]	[ ]	Attentive to details
[ ]	[ ]	Authentic
[ ]	[ ]	Broad-minded
[ ]	[ ]	Businesslike
[ ]	[ ]	Bold
[ ]	[ ]	Calm
[ ]	[ ]	Candid in dealing with others
[ ]	[ ]	Capable
[ ]	[ ]	Careful
[ ]	[ ]	Caring
[ ]	[ ]	Cautious
[ ]	[ ]	Challenge-seeking
[ ]	[ ]	Charismatic
[ ]	[ ]	Cheerful
[ ]	[ ]	Clear-thinking
[ ]	[ ]	Clever
[ ]	[ ]	Committed to personal growth
[ ]	[ ]	Communicative
[ ]	[ ]	Compassionate
[ ]	[ ]	Competent
[ ]	[ ]	Competitive
[ ]	[ ]	Concentration
[ ]	[ ]	Concern for others
[ ]	[ ]	Concise

[ ] [ ] Confident
[ ] [ ] Congenial
[ ] [ ] Conscientious
[ ] [ ] Conservative in thought
[ ] [ ] Considerate
[ ] [ ] Consistent
[ ] [ ] Cool under fire
[ ] [ ] Cooperative
[ ] [ ] Cost-conscious
[ ] [ ] Courageous
[ ] [ ] Creative
[ ] [ ] Credible
[ ] [ ] Curious
[ ] [ ] Daring
[ ] [ ] Decisive
[ ] [ ] Dedicated to organizations
[ ] [ ] Dedicated to personal goals
[ ] [ ] Deliberate
[ ] [ ] Demanding of self
[ ] [ ] Dependable
[ ] [ ] Detail-oriented
[ ] [ ] Determined
[ ] [ ] Dexterous
[ ] [ ] Diligent
[ ] [ ] Diplomatic
[ ] [ ] Direct
[ ] [ ] Discreet
[ ] [ ] Dynamic
[ ] [ ] Eager
[ ] [ ] Easily stimulated
[ ] [ ] Easygoing
[ ] [ ] Economical
[ ] [ ] Effective problem-solver
[ ] [ ] Efficient
[ ] [ ] Emotionally stable
[ ] [ ] Empathetic
[ ] [ ] Encouraging of others
[ ] [ ] Endurance
[ ] [ ] Energetic
[ ] [ ] Enterprising
[ ] [ ] Enthusiastic
[ ] [ ] Entrepreneurial
[ ] [ ] Exacting
[ ] [ ] Excited about challenge
[ ] [ ] Expressive
[ ] [ ] Factual
[ ] [ ] Fair-minded
[ ] [ ] Faithful
[ ] [ ] Farsighted
[ ] [ ] Fast-thinking on my feet

[ ] [ ] Firm
[ ] [ ] Flexible
[ ] [ ] Forceful
[ ] [ ] Foresight
[ ] [ ] Frank
[ ] [ ] Friendly
[ ] [ ] Frugal
[ ] [ ] Generous
[ ] [ ] Genuine
[ ] [ ] Goal-oriented
[ ] [ ] Good ego strength
[ ] [ ] Good follow-through
[ ] [ ] Good judgment
[ ] [ ] Good under stress
[ ] [ ] Gregarious
[ ] [ ] Hardworking
[ ] [ ] Healthy
[ ] [ ] Helpful
[ ] [ ] High energy
[ ] [ ] Honest
[ ] [ ] Humanistic
[ ] [ ] Idealistic
[ ] [ ] Imaginative
[ ] [ ] Independent
[ ] [ ] Individualistic
[ ] [ ] Industrious
[ ] [ ] Informal
[ ] [ ] Initiative
[ ] [ ] Innovative
[ ] [ ] Insightful
[ ] [ ] Insight into my own motives and behaviors
[ ] [ ] Integrity
[ ] [ ] Intellectual
[ ] [ ] Intelligent
[ ] [ ] In touch with my feelings
[ ] [ ] Introspective
[ ] [ ] Intuitive
[ ] [ ] Inventive
[ ] [ ] Involved
[ ] [ ] Kind
[ ] [ ] Knowledgeable about myself
[ ] [ ] Knowledgeable about the world
[ ] [ ] Levelheaded
[ ] [ ] Likable
[ ] [ ] Logical
[ ] [ ] Loving
[ ] [ ] Loyal
[ ] [ ] Mature

Acceptable	Needs Development	
[ ]	[ ]	Methodical
[ ]	[ ]	Meticulous
[ ]	[ ]	Modest
[ ]	[ ]	Moral
[ ]	[ ]	Motivated
[ ]	[ ]	Motivating
[ ]	[ ]	Natural
[ ]	[ ]	Neat and clean
[ ]	[ ]	Nurturing
[ ]	[ ]	Objective
[ ]	[ ]	Observant
[ ]	[ ]	Open to ideas
[ ]	[ ]	Open to others
[ ]	[ ]	Open-minded
[ ]	[ ]	Optimistic
[ ]	[ ]	Orderly
[ ]	[ ]	Organized
[ ]	[ ]	Original
[ ]	[ ]	Outgoing
[ ]	[ ]	Outspoken
[ ]	[ ]	Patient
[ ]	[ ]	People-oriented
[ ]	[ ]	Perceptive
[ ]	[ ]	Persevering
[ ]	[ ]	Persistent
[ ]	[ ]	Personable
[ ]	[ ]	Persuasive
[ ]	[ ]	Physically attractive
[ ]	[ ]	Physically strong
[ ]	[ ]	Playful
[ ]	[ ]	Poised
[ ]	[ ]	Polished
[ ]	[ ]	Politically aware
[ ]	[ ]	Positive
[ ]	[ ]	Practical
[ ]	[ ]	Precise
[ ]	[ ]	Proactive
[ ]	[ ]	Productive
[ ]	[ ]	Professional
[ ]	[ ]	Progressive
[ ]	[ ]	Project-oriented
[ ]	[ ]	Prudent
[ ]	[ ]	Punctual
[ ]	[ ]	Purposeful
[ ]	[ ]	Quick to take initiative
[ ]	[ ]	Rational
[ ]	[ ]	Realistic
[ ]	[ ]	Reasonable
[ ]	[ ]	Reflective
[ ]	[ ]	Relaxed

Acceptable	Needs Development	
[ ]	[ ]	Reliable
[ ]	[ ]	Reserved
[ ]	[ ]	Resilient
[ ]	[ ]	Resourceful
[ ]	[ ]	Responsible
[ ]	[ ]	Responsive
[ ]	[ ]	Results-oriented
[ ]	[ ]	Secure
[ ]	[ ]	Self-accepting
[ ]	[ ]	Self-analytical
[ ]	[ ]	Self-assured
[ ]	[ ]	Self-aware
[ ]	[ ]	Self-confident
[ ]	[ ]	Self-controlled
[ ]	[ ]	Self-correcting
[ ]	[ ]	Self-directed
[ ]	[ ]	Self-disciplined
[ ]	[ ]	Self-expressive
[ ]	[ ]	Self-improvement-oriented
[ ]	[ ]	Self-motivated
[ ]	[ ]	Self-reliant
[ ]	[ ]	Self-starting
[ ]	[ ]	Self-sufficient
[ ]	[ ]	Sensible
[ ]	[ ]	Sensitive to others
[ ]	[ ]	Sensitive to political climate
[ ]	[ ]	Serious-minded
[ ]	[ ]	Service-oriented
[ ]	[ ]	Shrewd
[ ]	[ ]	Sincere
[ ]	[ ]	Sociable
[ ]	[ ]	Socially adept
[ ]	[ ]	Sophisticated
[ ]	[ ]	Sound judgment
[ ]	[ ]	Spontaneous
[ ]	[ ]	Stable
[ ]	[ ]	Steady
[ ]	[ ]	Straightforward
[ ]	[ ]	Strong-willed (determined)
[ ]	[ ]	Supportive of others
[ ]	[ ]	Sympathetic
[ ]	[ ]	Systematic
[ ]	[ ]	Tactful
[ ]	[ ]	Task-oriented
[ ]	[ ]	Tenacious
[ ]	[ ]	Thorough
[ ]	[ ]	Thoughtful
[ ]	[ ]	Thoughtful of others
[ ]	[ ]	Thrifty
[ ]	[ ]	Tidy

[   ] [   ] Tolerant of ambiguity
[   ] [   ] Tolerant of others' mistakes
[   ] [   ] Tolerant of routine
[   ] [   ] Tough-minded
[   ] [   ] Trusting
[   ] [   ] Trustworthy
[   ] [   ] Unaffected
[   ] [   ] Unassuming
[   ] [   ] Understanding
[   ] [   ] Unexcitable
[   ] [   ] Uninhibited
[   ] [   ] Unpretentious
[   ] [   ] Unselfish
[   ] [   ] Venturesome
[   ] [   ] Verbal
[   ] [   ] Versatile
[   ] [   ] Warm
[   ] [   ] Well-groomed
[   ] [   ] Wholesome
[   ] [   ] Willing to learn
[   ] [   ] Willing to seek and take
          responsibility
[   ] [   ] Willing to work steadily for
          distant goals

[   ] [   ] Wise
[   ] [   ] Witty
[   ] [   ] _____
[   ] [   ] _____
[   ] [   ] _____
[   ] [   ] _____
[   ] [   ] _____
[   ] [   ] _____
[   ] [   ] _____
[   ] [   ] _____
[   ] [   ] _____
[   ] [   ] _____
[   ] [   ] _____
[   ] [   ] _____
[   ] [   ] _____
[   ] [   ] _____
[   ] [   ] _____
[   ] [   ] _____
[   ] [   ] _____
[   ] [   ] _____
[   ] [   ] _____
[   ] [   ] _____

[√] MOST IMPORTANT ADAPTIVE SKILLS CURRENTLY AT AN ACCEPTABLE LEVEL OF DEVELOPMENT

From the list that you just checked, select up to fifteen adaptive skills/personal qualities that you would most like to use in your worklife and that you consider to be currently at an acceptable level of development. If several adaptive skills appear the same or similar, group them together on a single line to form one cluster or family of related qualities. Use up to fifteen lines.

Priority   *Adaptive Skills*

[   ] _____

[   ] _____

[   ] _____

[   ] _____

[   ] _____

[   ] _____

[   ] _____

[   ] _____

[   ] _____

[   ] _____

[   ] _____

[   ] _____

[   ] _____

[   ] _____

[   ] _____

Write a 1 in the space to the left of the quality you consider to be your strongest, a 2 for the next most important quality, etc., until you have selected your five most important adaptive skills/personal qualities.

[√] MOST IMPORTANT ADAPTIVE SKILLS CURRENTLY IN NEED OF DEVELOPMENT

From the list that you just checked, select up to fifteen adaptive skills/ personal qualities that you would most like to use in your worklife and that you consider to need development. If several adaptive skills appear the same or similar, group them together on a single line to form one cluster or family of related qualities. Use up to fifteen lines.

Priority	*Adaptive Skills*
[ ]	_____
[ ]	_____
[ ]	_____
[ ]	_____
[ ]	_____
[ ]	_____
[ ]	_____
[ ]	_____
[ ]	_____
[ ]	_____
[ ]	_____
[ ]	_____
[ ]	_____
[ ]	_____
[ ]	_____

Write a 1 in the space to the left of the quality you consider to be most in need of development, a 2 for the next most important quality, etc., until you have selected your five most important adaptive skills/personal qualities currently in need of development.

6

INTERNAL BARRIERS

To be complete, any exploration of who you are must include an
inventory of internal barriers — those blocks, obstacles, or impediments
that keep you from being who you want to be, doing what you want
to do, and having what you want to have.

Problematic Personality Traits

These barriers commonly take the form of attitudes, behavior patterns, rigid
beliefs, fears, and real or imagined deficiencies in your skills, that somehow impede
your progress. While it may not be possible to eliminate all of these barriers, it is
possible to manage them or move ahead in spite of them. By admitting the
existence of a hampering characteristic or attitude, and observing how and when it
operates as a block, you can begin to modify the effects of any negative trait.

The first step is to tell the truth about your barriers, which you may find difficult or
upsetting! You must, however, accept yourself exactly as you are right now, for this
self-acceptance is the starting point of all self-improvement. Recognize that
everyone has barriers or attitude impediments, and that only those who are willing
to acknowledge them can deal with them effectively or eliminate them altogether.

Internal barriers can be reflective of your individual style characteristics. Compare
your internal barriers with your style and career type. Try to determine whether
certain attitudes stem from your work type or can accurately be termed personal
deficiencies you want to overcome.

Assessing Your Internal Barriers

Read through the list of internal barriers and problematic personality
characteristics on the following pages and check those that you feel currently give
you difficulty on your job or in your life. Space is provided for you to add any
barriers that have not been included on the list.

Again, this list has been developed with some redundancy or overlap, as there are
various ways of expressing the qualities or attitudes that can constitute an internal

barrier. It's most important that you recognize and acknowledge them. Don't be alarmed: most people check over twenty-five internal barriers applicable to themselves!

If in the course of getting in touch with your internal barriers you do become troubled or depressed, we would encourage you to seek professional counseling in dealing with your feelings. Counseling can enable you to maximize your potential for happiness, fulfillment, and professional satisfaction.

Further references on self-improvement and dealing with barriers on your own are included in the selected reading materials at the end of this book.

[✓] INTERNAL BARRIERS

Remember, check only those barriers that currently give you difficulty in your worklife.

"I tend to be [or have or suffer from] . . ."

[ ] A show-off
[ ] A workaholic
[ ] Abrasive
[ ] Abrupt
[ ] Absentminded
[ ] "All-or-nothing" behavior
[ ] Aloof
[ ] Ambivalent
[ ] An unclear sense of identity
[ ] An underachiever
[ ] Anger (uncontrolled)
[ ] Antisocial
[ ] Anxious
[ ] Apathetic
[ ] Argumentative
[ ] Arrogant
[ ] Autocratic
[ ] Bitter
[ ] "Black or white" thinking
[ ] Blaming of others
[ ] Boastful
[ ] Boring
[ ] Bossy and dominating
[ ] Burnt-out
[ ] Careless
[ ] Closed-minded
[ ] Coarse
[ ] Coldhearted
[ ] Complaining
[ ] Compulsive
[ ] Conceited
[ ] Conflicting values
[ ] Confrontational
[ ] Confused self-image
[ ] Constricted
[ ] Cynical

[ ] Deceitful
[ ] Defensive
[ ] Delusional
[ ] Depressed often
[ ] Dictatorial
[ ] Difficulty being competitive
[ ] Difficulty being concise
[ ] Difficulty developing reasonable personal expectations
[ ] Difficulty expressing anger
[ ] Difficulty expressing feelings in general
[ ] Difficulty generating alternatives
[ ] Difficulty getting organized
[ ] Difficulty listening well
[ ] Difficulty making decisions
[ ] Difficulty managing details
[ ] Difficulty managing stress and pressure
[ ] Difficulty managing time
[ ] Difficulty planning ahead
[ ] Difficulty relating well to others
[ ] Difficulty selling myself
[ ] Difficulty setting priorities
[ ] Difficulty sustaining concentration
[ ] Difficulty with ambiguity or uncertainty
[ ] Difficulty with authority
[ ] Difficulty with lack of structure
[ ] Difficulty with rejection
[ ] Difficulty with structure
[ ] Difficulty with taking criticism
[ ] Diffuse and scattered
[ ] Disorganized
[ ] Distrustful of others

[ ] Dogmatic
[ ] Dull and overly methodical
[ ] Easily bored
[ ] Easily discouraged
[ ] Easily distracted
[ ] Easily frustrated
[ ] Easily hurt feelings
[ ] Easily irritated
[ ] Easily overwhelmed
[ ] Egocentric
[ ] Egotistical
[ ] Envious
[ ] Erratic
[ ] Excessive concern with what others think of me
[ ] Excessive daydreams and fantasies
[ ] Excessive distrust of intuition
[ ] Excessive distrust of others
[ ] Excessive distrust of technology
[ ] Excessive guilt feelings
[ ] Excessive need for approval
[ ] Excessive need for attention
[ ] Excessive need for certainty
[ ] Excessive need for control
[ ] Excessive need for external validation
[ ] Excessive need for security
[ ] Excessive need to please others
[ ] Excessively competitive
[ ] Excessively compulsive
[ ] Excessively demanding of myself
[ ] Excessively fault-finding
[ ] Excessively self-critical
[ ] Excessively self-involved
[ ] Fear masquerading as laziness
[ ] Fear of age limitations
[ ] Fear of appearing weak
[ ] Fear of authority
[ ] Fear of being at financial risk
[ ] Fear of being myself
[ ] Fear of change
[ ] Fear of closing options
[ ] Fear of commitment
[ ] Fear of competition
[ ] Fear of failure
[ ] Fear of financial insecurity
[ ] Fear of hurting others
[ ] Fear of looking foolish
[ ] Fear of losing
[ ] Fear of making mistakes
[ ] Fear of promotion
[ ] Fear of public speaking
[ ] Fear of risk-taking
[ ] Fear of success
[ ] Fear of taking responsibility

[ ] Fear of technology
[ ] Fear of the unknown
[ ] Feelings of being an imposter or fraud
[ ] Feelings of being unsophisticated
[ ] Feelings of inadequacy
[ ] Frequent feelings of being a victim
[ ] Financial insecurity
[ ] Flighty
[ ] Forgetful
[ ] Fussy
[ ] Generally fearful
[ ] Generous to a fault
[ ] Greedy
[ ] Hardheaded
[ ] Haughty
[ ] High-strung
[ ] Hostile toward others
[ ] Hypersensitive
[ ] Immature
[ ] Impatient
[ ] Impossible
[ ] Impulsive
[ ] Inability to self-evaluate performance
[ ] Inconsistent
[ ] Indecisive
[ ] Indiscreet
[ ] Inflexible
[ ] Inhibiting self-doubt
[ ] Insensitive to needs and feelings of others
[ ] Intolerant
[ ] Irresponsible
[ ] Irritable
[ ] Irritatingly offbeat
[ ] Jealous
[ ] Lack of assertiveness
[ ] Lack of confidence
[ ] Lack of diplomacy
[ ] Lack of follow-through
[ ] Lack of goals
[ ] Lack of motivation
[ ] Lack of persistence
[ ] Lack of social skills
[ ] Lack of spontaneity
[ ] Lack of tact
[ ] Lack of vision
[ ] Lazy
[ ] Limited attention span
[ ] Low frustration tolerance
[ ] Low self-esteem
[ ] Low stress tolerance
[ ] Manipulative

[ ] Meek
[ ] Moody
[ ] Naive politically
[ ] Naive socially
[ ] Narcissistic
[ ] Need for excessive positive
    reinforcement from others
[ ] Need for guarantees
[ ] Need for immediate gratification
[ ] Need to compare self to others
[ ] Negative self-concept
[ ] Negativistic
[ ] Nervous
[ ] Nosy
[ ] Obnoxious
[ ] Out of touch with my feelings
[ ] Out to lunch
[ ] Overly aggressive
[ ] Overly anxious to please
[ ] Overly blunt
[ ] Overly cautious
[ ] Overly compliant
[ ] Overly concerned with details
[ ] Overly controlled
[ ] Overly controlling of others
[ ] Overly critical
[ ] Overly dependent
[ ] Overly detached
[ ] Overly eager to impress others
[ ] Overly emotional
[ ] Overly inhibited
[ ] Overly judgmental
[ ] Overly opinionated
[ ] Overly passive
[ ] Overly pessimistic
[ ] Overly reactive
[ ] Overly ready to take on guilt
[ ] Overly restricting belief systems
[ ] Overly skeptical
[ ] Overly suggestible
[ ] Overly talkative
[ ] Overly task-oriented
[ ] Overly temperamental
[ ] Overly trusting
[ ] Paranoid
[ ] Perfectionism
[ ] Physical fear
[ ] Plateaued
[ ] Poor ego strength
[ ] Poor judge of other people
[ ] Poor listening skills
[ ] Poor physical health
[ ] Poor self-control
[ ] Poor self-discipline
[ ] Poor self-management

[ ] Poor sense of appropriate
    appearance
[ ] Prejudiced
[ ] Preoccupied with self
[ ] Problems being competitive
[ ] Procrastination
[ ] Prone to vacillation
[ ] Quick to anger
[ ] Reactive instead of proactive
[ ] Rebellious
[ ] Resistance to new ideas and
    people
[ ] Restless
[ ] Rigid
[ ] Sarcastic
[ ] Self-denying
[ ] Self-doubt
[ ] Self-indulgent
[ ] Self-pitying
[ ] Self-sabotaging
[ ] Selfish
[ ] Sense of lack of creativity
[ ] Shallow
[ ] Short-tempered
[ ] "Should or ought" thinking
[ ] Shy to an extreme
[ ] Skeptical
[ ] Slow to forgive
[ ] Slow to see humor
[ ] Smug
[ ] Snobbish
[ ] Socially awkward
[ ] Stubborn
[ ] Stingy
[ ] Strong need to prove myself
[ ] Submissive
[ ] Substance abuse
[ ] Sulky
[ ] Suspicious of others' motives
[ ] Tendency to blow up regularly
[ ] Tendency to delay or avoid action
[ ] Tendency to hold everything in
[ ] Tendency to keep people at a
    distance and avoid close
    relationships
[ ] Tendency to obsess about things
[ ] Tendency to personalize things
[ ] Tendency to take path of least
    resistance
[ ] Tendency to vacillate
[ ] Tense
[ ] Thin-skinned
[ ] Tight control over feelings and
    emotions
[ ] Timid

[ ] Too ready to avoid conflict
[ ] Touchy
[ ] Unaware of my impact on others
[ ] Undependable
[ ] Uneasy about physical appearance
[ ] Uninterested in others
[ ] Uninvolved
[ ] Unmotivated
[ ] Unrealistic
[ ] Unrealistic expectation of others
[ ] Unrealistic expectation of myself
[ ] Unreasonable
[ ] Unresponsive
[ ] Untidy
[ ] Values conflicts
[ ] Vindictive
[ ] Vulnerable to real or imagined
    threats

[ ] Withdrawn
[ ] Worrisome
[ ] _____
[ ] _____
[ ] _____
[ ] _____
[ ] _____
[ ] _____
[ ] _____
[ ] _____
[ ] _____
[ ] _____
[ ] _____
[ ] _____
[ ] _____
[ ] _____
[ ] _____

[√] MOST IMPORTANT INTERNAL BARRIERS CURRENTLY IN NEED OF REDUCTION OR ELIMINATION

From the list that you just checked, select up to fifteen work-related internal barriers that you would most like to reduce or eliminate from your work or life. If several words are similar in meaning, group them together and include them on a single line to form a cluster or family of internal barriers. Use up to fifteen lines.

Priority: ***Internal Barriers***

[   ] _____

[   ] _____

[   ] _____

[   ] _____

[   ] _____

[   ] _____

[   ] _____

[   ] _____

[   ] _____

[   ] _____

[   ] _____

[   ] _____

[   ] _____

[   ] _____

[   ] _____

Write a 1 in the space to the left of the barrier you consider to be your greatest work-related internal barrier, a 2 for the next most important barrier, etc., until you have identified your five most important work-related internal barriers currently in need of reduction or elimination.

7

MOTIVATION
(PART 2) VALUES AND NEEDS

Your Career Values and Needs

This final inventory explores your values and needs—the essential, driving forces in your life. Howard Figler, in *The Complete Job-Search Handbook*, defined work values as "those enduring dimensions or aspects of our work that we regard as important sources of satisfaction."

Some values we hold strongly, others less so. In the career values and needs assessment that follows, you will examine your own work values and determine how important each of them is to you. This exercise, sometimes called "values clarification," will give you further insight into what motivates you in your worklife.

Need is defined in the dictionary as a necessity, a requirement, a demand, or even a pressing lack of something essential. Thus, needs take on a somewhat stronger sense of urgency than do values. Often, however, our values are reflections of underlying needs; and sometimes it's difficult to distinguish between those elements of experience that we value and those that we need. The assessment provided here treats needs and values together in a single instrument.

Assessing Your Career Values and Needs

The items in this inventory are designed to help you identify the career values and needs that are most important to you in your worklife. As you check this inventory, try to dig deep into what really matters to you. Remember, there are no right or wrong answers—only your answers.

For each of the values and needs listed, check whether it is important, neutral, or unimportant to your worklife satisfaction.

	Important	Neutral	Unimportant
1. Achievement To have the opportunity to excel and produce significant results, setting high standards for myself and doing work that is challenging.	[ ]	[ ]	[ ]
2. Advancement To have my work lead to better opportunities for greater responsibility.	[ ]	[ ]	[ ]
3. Adventure/Excitement To have work in which I am frequently excited about the activities or results, and take some risks.	[ ]	[ ]	[ ]
4. Aesthetics To be involved in work that deals with creating or studying beautiful things.	[ ]	[ ]	[ ]
5. Affiliation To identify myself and be recognized as belonging to a specific company or organization where I can develop close personal relationships or friendships.	[ ]	[ ]	[ ]
6. Artistic Creativity To create objects, images, or other products of my own work in an art form.	[ ]	[ ]	[ ]
7. Attractive Environment To work in an environment that I find attractive and comfortable to be in.	[ ]	[ ]	[ ]
8. Challenging Problems To work frequently on issues and problems that will challenge my ability.	[ ]	[ ]	[ ]
9. Change and Variety To have work that varies frequently in form, content, or location.	[ ]	[ ]	[ ]
10. Close to Power To have a position where I am in touch with the seats of power, where I have direct and frequent contact with influential people, where I contribute to making big decisions.	[ ]	[ ]	[ ]
11. Community To be involved in the affairs of the community in which I live.	[ ]	[ ]	[ ]
12. Competition To work at jobs where I can test my abilities to win over others.	[ ]	[ ]	[ ]

13. **Control**   [ ]   [ ]   [ ]

   To be in a position where I am in as much control of my workday as possible.

14. **Creative Expression**   [ ]   [ ]   [ ]

   To create new concepts, products, services, structures, systems, etc. that do not follow established rules, procedures, and patterns.

15. **Ethics**   [ ]   [ ]   [ ]

   To perform activities and work in an environment consistent with my moral principles and which do not violate my personal beliefs.

16. **Exercise Competence**   [ ]   [ ]   [ ]

   To demonstrate that I do excellent work, understand my job well, and am a competent and effective person.

17. **External Structure**   [ ]   [ ]   [ ]

   To work in an environment that provides structure in the form of broad guidelines to follow, objectives to achieve, and clear expectations. To have clear parameters under which to operate.

18. **Exhibition**   [ ]   [ ]   [ ]

   To have an audience or group of people whose attention I command.

19. **Fame**   [ ]   [ ]   [ ]

   To be well known to a very large number of people for the quality of the work I do.

20. **Fast Pace**   [ ]   [ ]   [ ]

   To work in an environment where results need to be produced quickly and on schedule.

21. **Field of Strong Interest**   [ ]   [ ]   [ ]

   To work in a field of major importance to me where I can perform activities of intrinsic interest.

22. **Help Society**   [ ]   [ ]   [ ]

   To work in a way that perceptibly benefits society.

23. **High Earnings**   [ ]   [ ]   [ ]

   To have an income that provides me with plenty of discretionary funds.

24. **Independence and Autonomy**   [ ]   [ ]   [ ]

   To be able to work without being told what to do or having to report back frequently.

25. **Influence People**   [ ]   [ ]   [ ]

To have a position in which I affect how people think.

26. **Intellectual Status**   [ ]   [ ]   [ ]

To have others appreciate me as a person with high intelligence or as an expert in a specific field.

27. **Job Tranquility**   [ ]   [ ]   [ ]

To work in an environment relatively free of stress and pressure.

28. **Knowledge**   [ ]   [ ]   [ ]

To work in the pursuit of increased learning, professional development, and understanding in my field of expertise.

29. **Leadership**   [ ]   [ ]   [ ]

To be the person to whom others look for vision and direction.

30. **Leisure**   [ ]   [ ]   [ ]

To have enough time to pursue activities of importance to me outside of work.

31. **Location**   [ ]   [ ]   [ ]

To live in a place that allows me to pursue my lifestyle fully and easily, and provides easy access to my place of work.

32. **Make Decisions**   [ ]   [ ]   [ ]

To be in a position to make decisions that affect the quality and successful outcome of projects.

33. **Nurturing and Helping Others**   [ ]   [ ]   [ ]

To be involved in work that allows me to be supportive and understanding of others: teaching, helping, guiding, curing, or otherwise providing a direct service to others.

34. **Order**   [ ]   [ ]   [ ]

To keep personal effects, surroundings, and work structures neat and organized, and work in an environment where things are done in a planned, systematic, and orderly manner.

35. **Physical Challenge**   [ ]   [ ]   [ ]

To have a physically demanding and rewarding job.

36. **Play**   [ ]   [ ]   [ ]

To do things "just for fun" and spend time participating in games, sports, and other social activities and amusements. To maintain a lighthearted, easygoing attitude toward life.

37. ***Power and Authority***   [ ]   [ ]   [ ]

    To be in a position to control the work and the organizational future of others.

38. ***Precision Work***   [ ]   [ ]   [ ]

    To perform work in which making precise measurements or working with finely detailed objects is important and avoiding errors is critical.

39. ***Prestige/Recognition***   [ ]   [ ]   [ ]

    To do work that others consider to be important and to be recognized for the quality of my work.

40. ***Profit, Gain***   [ ]   [ ]   [ ]

    To have my work exercise a strong influence on the bottom line.

41. ***Public Contact***   [ ]   [ ]   [ ]

    To work face-to-face with the public.

42. ***Respect from Others***   [ ]   [ ]   [ ]

    To have others look on my ability with respect.

43. ***Security***   [ ]   [ ]   [ ]

    To know that I will keep my job and continue to receive reasonable compensation.

44. ***Stability***   [ ]   [ ]   [ ]

    To do work that changes little over long periods of time and is predictable.

45. ***Status***   [ ]   [ ]   [ ]

    To have friends, family, and the community look at me with respect for my position.

46. ***Supportive Environment/Supportive Supervisor***   [ ]   [ ]   [ ]

    To work for a receptive boss/employer to whom I can comfortably turn for advice, counsel, help, and support.

47. ***Time Freedom***   [ ]   [ ]   [ ]

    To keep my own schedule and be able to work at my own pace without pressure from others.

48. ***Work Alone***   [ ]   [ ]   [ ]

    To produce results with little or no contact or input from others.

49. *Work on Frontiers of Knowledge*   [ ]   [ ]   [ ]

To generate new ideas, develop new technology, work at the forefront of social or physical science, or otherwise work on the cutting edge of my field.

50. *Work Under Pressure*   [ ]   [ ]   [ ]

To work in situations demanding high concentration under time pressure over long periods of time with little margin for error.

51. *Work with Others*   [ ]   [ ]   [ ]

To work with other people toward common goals in a cooperative team effort.

Add any values or needs that may not have been included on the list that you feel are important to you.

52. _____

53. _____

54. _____

55. _____

56. _____

57. _____

58. _____

[√] IMPORTANT CAREER VALUES AND NEEDS

In the spaces provided below, list those values and needs that you checked as important, plus those you added. For each value or need that you write below, decide whether your current worklife satisfies that value or need. Where you feel that one or more needs or values overlap in their meaning for you, either pick the ones that best expresses that need or value for you or list them all on one line.

	Value or Need	*Currently Satisfied*	*Not Yet Satisfied*
1.		[ ]	[ ]
2.		[ ]	[ ]
3.		[ ]	[ ]
4.		[ ]	[ ]
5.		[ ]	[ ]
6.		[ ]	[ ]
7.		[ ]	[ ]
8.		[ ]	[ ]
9.		[ ]	[ ]
10.		[ ]	[ ]
11.		[ ]	[ ]
12.		[ ]	[ ]
13.		[ ]	[ ]
14.		[ ]	[ ]
15.		[ ]	[ ]
16.		[ ]	[ ]

	Currently Satisfied	Not Yet Satisfied
17. _____	[ ]	[ ]
18. _____	[ ]	[ ]
19. _____	[ ]	[ ]
20. _____	[ ]	[ ]
21. _____	[ ]	[ ]
22. _____	[ ]	[ ]
23. _____	[ ]	[ ]
24. _____	[ ]	[ ]
25. _____	[ ]	[ ]
26. _____	[ ]	[ ]
27. _____	[ ]	[ ]
28. _____	[ ]	[ ]
29. _____	[ ]	[ ]
30. _____	[ ]	[ ]
31. _____	[ ]	[ ]
32. _____	[ ]	[ ]
33. _____	[ ]	[ ]

[√] MOST IMPORTANT VALUES AND NEEDS CURRENTLY SATISFIED

From the list you developed above, select up to fifteen values and needs that you consider to be the most important to have in your worklife to insure your satisfaction and/or success and that *are* currently satisfied in your worklife, and write them in the spaces provided below. Where you feel that one or more needs or values overlap in their meaning for you, either pick the one that best expresses that need or value for you or list them all on one line. Use up to fifteen lines.

Priority: *Values and Needs*

[　] _____

[　] _____

[　] _____

[　] _____

[　] _____

[　] _____

[　] _____

[　] _____

[　] _____

[　] _____

[　] _____

[　] _____

[　] _____

[　] _____

[　] _____

Write a 1 in the box to the left of the value or need you consider to be your highest priority, a 2 for the next most important value or need, etc., until you have selected five values or needs you consider most important to you.

[✓] MOST IMPORTANT VALUES AND NEEDS NOT YET SATISFIED

From the list you developed above, select up to fifteen values and needs that you consider to be the most important to have in your worklife to ensure your satisfaction and/or success and *are not yet* satisfied in your worklife, and write them in the spaces provided below. Where you feel that one or more needs or values overlap in their meaning for you, either pick the one that best expresses that need or value for you or list them all on one line. Use up to fifteen lines.

Priority   *Values and Needs*

[   ] _____

[   ] _____

[   ] _____

[   ] _____

[   ] _____

[   ] _____

[   ] _____

[   ] _____

[   ] _____

[   ] _____

[   ] _____

[   ] _____

[   ] _____

[   ] _____

[   ] _____

Write a 1 in the box to the left of the value or need you consider to be your highest priority, a 2 for the next most important value or need, etc., until you have selected five values or needs you consider most important to you that are not yet satisfied.

8

PERSONAL CAREER PROFILE

You have put a significant amount of work into this battery of
assessments in order to discover who you are in relation to your worklife.
Now it will be extremely valuable for you to put all the information
together in a concise, readable, and usable way.

The *Personal Career Profile*® has been developed for just that purpose, to
allow you to refer to a single document that clearly expresses who you
are. The Personal Career Profile is not a résumé. It does not contain your
work history or education. But, like a multidimensional X-ray or "career
CAT-scan," it provides you with a deeper image of yourself in
relation to your career and worklife.

Your Concise Personal Career Profile

The two-page spread on pages 88 and 89 will be used to create a concise version of
your Personal Career Profile. A more detailed version will follow. Complete the
concise form as follows:

1. **Style.** Write the four-letter code for your work type (from page 24) in the four
   boxes provided. In the lines provided, write in five key words or phrases from
   your summary (from page 44) that you consider best describe your style.

2. **Career Type.** Write the three-letter Holland code for your career type (from
   page 51) in the three boxes provided. In the lines provided, write in five key
   words or phrases from that summary (from page 52) that you feel best describe
   your types.

3. **Career Interests.** From page 53, write in your five most appealing
   occupations, job titles, or broad areas of work.

4. **Motivation.** In the spaces provided, write the five preferences for people,
   places, jobs, and cultures that you indicated on pages 9, 10, 13, and 15. From
   page 85, write in your five most important values and needs currently satisfied.

Concise Personal Career Profile

This diagram or concise profile serves as a one-page overview and will function as an outline for your final narrative-form profile.

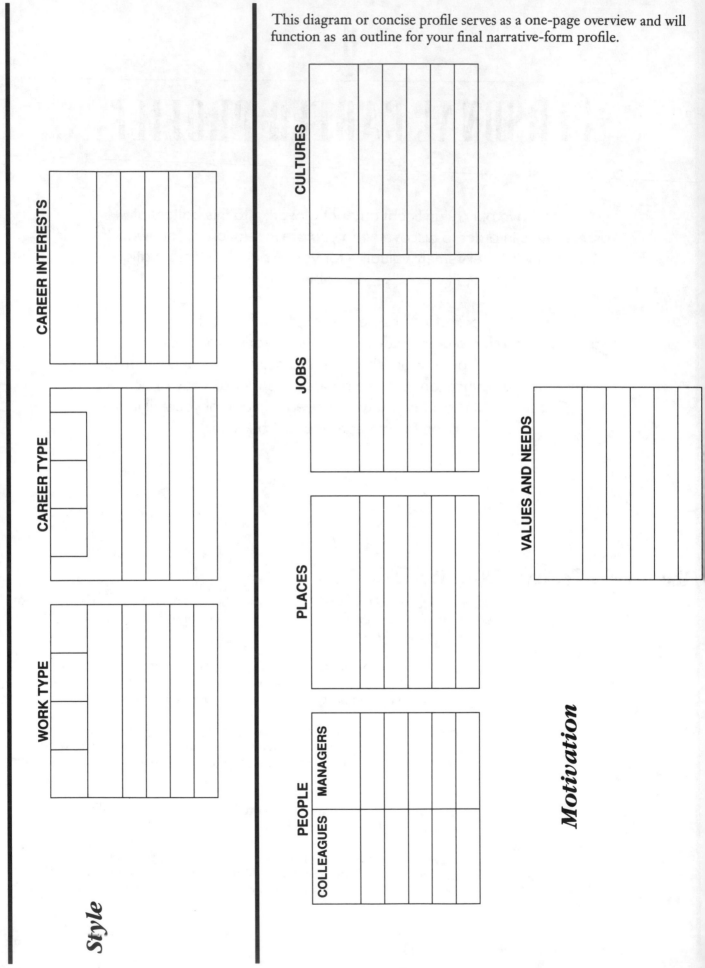

Style

WORK TYPE

CAREER TYPE

CAREER INTERESTS

PEOPLE

COLLEAGUES | MANAGERS

PLACES

JOBS

CULTURES

Motivation

VALUES AND NEEDS

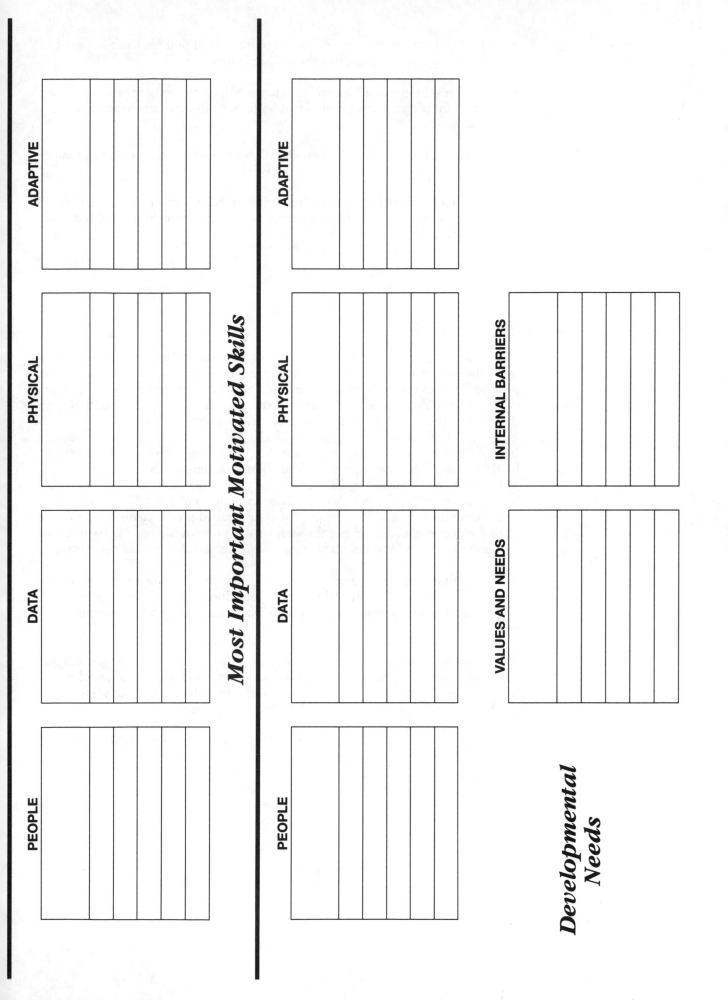

Most Important Motivated Skills

PEOPLE   DATA   PHYSICAL   ADAPTIVE

PEOPLE   DATA   PHYSICAL   ADAPTIVE

VALUES AND NEEDS   INTERNAL BARRIERS

Developmental Needs

5. **Most Important Motivated Skills.** From pages 61 and 68, write in your five most important people, data, physical, and adaptive skills.

6. **Skill Developmental Needs.** From pages 62 and 69, write in your five most important people, data, physical and adaptive skills currently in need of development.

7. **Values and Needs Not Yet Satisfied.** From page 86, write in your five most important values and needs not yet satisfied.

8. **Internal Barriers in Need of Reduction or Elimination.** From page 76, write in your five most serious internal barriers currently in need of reduction or elimination.

Your Detailed Personal Career Profile

The principal format is a narrative description of you in relation to your worklife, using the information you discovered in the assessments along with the descriptions provided of the various styles and types and any other ideas, thoughts, or feelings that arise as you write the profile. Specific career interests have been omitted from the detailed profile examples, but you may include them if you wish.

It's a good idea to read one or more of the examples first, which follow on pages 92–105, before you write your final detailed profile. Remember that the samples provided are not intended to describe precisely every person who holds the job title for which the profile has been written. It is perfectly appropriate if you are a mid-level corporate manager, for example, for your detailed profile to differ significantly from the one provided here! But the samples will give you a sense of how to create a cohesive narrative from the material that has emerged from the assessments.

Take your time putting the profile together. Follow the directions carefully, work on drafts, and make sure you are satisfied with your final version. Take liberties with the format if doing so provides you with a clearer and more useful description of your profile.

Write your drafts on a word processor if you have access to one, since you will want to be able to revise them as easily as possible. When you finish a draft, read it through several times. Revise your profile until it tells the truth about you—until you can recognize yourself and say, "Yes, that is really me!"

When you've done this, you'll feel a new sense of satisfaction and self-recognition, and you'll be on your way to knowing and being *who you are*.

Instructions for Completing Your Detailed Personal Career Profile

Refer to the examples for clarification of any of these instructions. Use your Concise Personal Career Profile for quick retrieval of information. Write as much as you feel necessary to describe yourself fully and with satisfaction.

1. **Style.** Use the summary you wrote on page 44. If you have not yet written this summary, refer to the instructions on that page.

2. **Career Type.** Again, use the summary you wrote on page 52, or if you haven't written it yet, refer to the instructions on that page.

3. **Preferences.** In four simple sentences, summarize the five people, places, jobs, and cultures preferences that you included in your concise personal career profile.

4. **Values and Needs.** In a single sentence, state your five most important values and needs. Add some remarks about what you are doing to include those values in your worklife. Then discuss in one sentence your five most important values and needs not yet satisfied.

5. **Functional Skills.** State briefly your five most important people, data, and physical skills that you currently consider to be at an acceptable level of development. Then write a sentence that states the five most important people, data, and physical skills that you feel are most in need of development.

6. **Adaptive Skills.** In a single sentence, state your five most important adaptive skills/personal qualities that you consider to be at an acceptable level of development in your present work experience. Then write a sentence mentioning the five most important adaptive skills that you feel are in need of development.

7. **Internal Barriers.** State plainly the five most serious or troublesome internal barriers that you feel are currently in need of reduction or elimination for more success and satisfaction in your worklife.

The following sample profiles will give you a sense of how all of the information from the assessments can be condensed in a readable manner.

Entrepreneur/Small Business Owner:

Style:

My work type is ENTJ and my style is that of the "intuitive, innovative organizer." I enjoy being an executive and running my own business. I like to think ahead, organize plans, and make a systematic effort to reach my objectives on schedule. I have always sought leadership roles, am frank in my expression, and have tried to be innovative in creating a vision for the future of organizations to which I belong. I like to be well-informed and enjoy adding to my fund of knowledge.

Career Type:

My primary career type is investigative. I am comfortable with abstractions, enjoy solving problems through the use of my analytical skills, love learning new things, and like to understand clearly how things work. I have been successful in an engineering job and have also worked as an engineering professor. In my current job, I am drawn to using computers and creating systems. My secondary career type is enterprising. I am adventurous and drawn to power and leadership roles. I consider myself aggressive and self-confident, and have demonstrated social, leadership, and speaking abilities. I have worked my way to the top of nearly every organization in which I have worked. My teritary career type is social. I am interested in other people and consider myself sensitive to their needs. I have taught professionally and value interpersonal relations. I often use my verbal and social skills to sell products and services to other people. I am cheerful, sometimes impulsive, and verbally oriented.

Preferences:

I prefer most of the people with whom I work to be critical and demanding of excellence from themselves and me, interested in getting their own work done without a lot of interaction with others, well above average in intelligence (and skill levels), and zealous about the company. I like to work in a quiet, low-key office in my own home, where I can use my own pictures and things and where there are windows looking out on an interesting view. I like to acquire new skills, write nonfiction books, advertising copy, and workbooks, and meet new people. I prefer my company to be a small intimate group, competitive, demanding, very stable, and explorative.

Values and Needs:

My most important values include independence, full self-expression, creative expression, challenging problems, and high earnings. I am attempting to include these values in my work by owning my own business and spending as much time as possible in the area of developing new products through the exercise of my creative abilities. The values and needs that I want to bring into more focus in my life include prestige and recognition, intellectual status, job tranquility, knowledge, and leadership.

Functional Skills:

My most important functional skills are working with abstract material and concepts, communicating abstract concepts, envisioning the future, writing narratives, and organizing information logically. I am attempting to use these motivated skills in my work by spending as much time as possible writing materials that describe abstract ideas in such a way that people can easily grasp them and use them in their own lives. The skills that I need and want to develop to be more successful include acting assertively, managing people, persuading others, allocating resources, and monitoring and regulating work flow.

Adaptive Skills:

The personal qualities that work best for me include being ambitious, committed to personal growth, confident, creative, and hardworking. I need to work more on being assertive, demanding of others, methodical, persuasive, and caring.

Internal Barriers:

The key barriers that inhibit my success include lack of assertiveness, being reactive instead of proactive, fear of not knowing, impatience, and restlessness. These developmental needs all relate to my need to do a better job building my business and developing and managing the people that work for me.

Mid-Level Corporate Manager:

Style:

My work type is ESTJ and my style is that of the "fact-minded, practical organizer." I like to organize projects and make sure they are completed. I like being a manager and like to work with people who are focused on getting the job done in a structured environment where there are rewards available for succeeding. I deal with people in a direct way with consistency and fairness. I consider myself to be loyal and dependable.

Career Type:

My primary career type is conventional. I like to be accurate and responsible as well as practical in working and making decisions. I enjoy working on teams and both leading and making a significant contribution. I do not prefer a lot of change in my environment. My secondary career type is enterprising. I can be aggressive and hard-driving when there is a job that needs to get done. I communicate well with my staff. I have always been valued as a key manager in my company, where I have worked for over ten years. My tertiary career type is realistic. I spend my off-work hours in my garden and working around the house, and I take pride in being able to make minor repairs on my own car. At work, I have always been considered to be very practical, "hands-on," and technically capable.

Preferences:

I want to work with people who are well above average in skill levels, constantly pressing toward higher levels of performance, and practical and down-to-earth. I prefer my manager to be ready to give feedback whenever necessary and someone who leads from behind. I like to work indoors in the same place every day, in a private office where I can concentrate on my work and where everything is well appointed, in place, and supplied by the company. I like to build and lead teams, manage people, solve organizational problems, and work with young people. I want my company to be competitive, hard-driving, traditional, powerful, and worldwide.

Values and Needs:

The most important values and needs currently satisfied in my worklife include affiliation, challenging problems, respect from others, achievement, and security. I would like to see the following values and needs better satisfied in my worklife and need to focus my attention so I can bring these into fruition: prestige/recognition, advancement, community, independence, and high earnings.

Functional Skills:

I consider my top functional skills to be managing people, working effectively on a team, synthesizing facts and ideas, coordinating events and operations, and solving problems. I use these almost every day in my work and have seen significant growth in my mastery of these skills. I need development in acknowledging others, resolving conflict, listening attentively, showing warmth and respect, and operating a computer terminal. I plan to give more attention to these shortcomings through courses and through focusing on developing these skills on the job.

Adaptive Skills:

My top adaptive skills include being attentive to details, strong-willed, self-correcting, perceptive, and industrious. These have been extremely useful to me throughout my career not only as a manager, but also when I was working my way up the ladder. I need development in being spontaneous, concerned about people, expressive, dynamic, and open to others. I am uncertain about how to deal with these and will seek professional guidance through course work or reading.

Internal Barriers:

I would like to eliminate or reduce the following internal barriers: lack of diplomacy, stubbornness, impatience, insensitivity to needs and feelings of others, and being confrontational with others.

Corporate Administrator:

Style:

My work type is ISTJ and my style is that of the "analytical manager of facts and details." I am practical, logical, dependable, orderly, matter-of-fact, and well-organized. Every job I have had has been one that requires my being well-organized and able to work with numbers or other detailed pieces of information that have to be remembered, analyzed, put into the right place, and properly categorized. I get a lot of pleasure from managing in an orderly, well-structured, and stable environment without too many surprises.

Career Type:

My primary career type is conventional. I have a small group of long-term close friends with whom I spend time and share common life experiences. I want the people I work with to be orderly and to pay attention to the structure and rules of the organization. I also like my own work to be accurate and practical. I don't like flashy people, ideas, or ways of working. My secondary career type is investigative. I am analytical in my thinking and enjoy solving problems where I have to use my head to think through the solutions. I have faithful and long-term relationships with a small number of close friends and colleagues. I like to work on teams as long as I am free to make my individual contribution without too much distraction from others. My tertiary career type is artistic. I read extensively in the arts, attend the theater on a regular basis, and have even acted in community and college theater. When I retire, I would love to be involved in the theater, even as an amateur.

Preferences:

I much prefer to be around people who are passive, slow-moving, and quiet, interested in maintaining their own standards and leaving me to mine, satisfied with getting their jobs done and meeting standard goals, and able to turn out very large amounts of work day after day. I want my manager to be willing to let me do things my own way as long as the results are achieved. I prefer working indoors, in a quiet low-key, commercial office in the city, where I can use my own pictures and other things. I like to calculate taxes, carry out detailed instructions, do cost accounting, classify and categorize information, and maintain financial records. I most like to work in a company that is corporate-conservative, peaceful, environmentally conscious, very stable, and dedicated to making money.

Values and Needs:

The most important values and needs currently satisfied in my worklife include order, security, job tranquility, location, and challenging problems. My current job satisfies those needs. They are important enough to me that I would change companies if they could not be satisfied. Those areas that are not yet satisfied include stability, time freedom, working alone, intellectual status, and leisure. I believe that I am working toward the satisfaction of these needs as I grow in my present job and in the company.

Functional Skills:

My most important functional skills include administering policy and programs, organizing information logically, negotiating contracts, keeping records, and thinking logically. I use these continuously on my current job and would want to continue using these skills wherever I worked. The functional skills that I consider to be most in need of development include relating to a wide variety of people, communicating effectively, using statistics, delegating responsibility, and resolving conflicts. I also feel that here, as in the values and needs area, that these skills will be developed as I grow in my job and the company.

Adaptive Skills:

My most important adaptive skills include being hardworking, organized, self-disciplined, steady, and reliable. I need to work on improving in being more open to others, imaginative, concerned about people, demanding of others, and a better team player.

Internal Barriers:

The internal barriers that I feel can hold me back the most and that I need to give attention to overcoming include difficulty with taking criticism, black-or-white thinking, difficulty selling myself, being easily irritated, and inflexibility.

Senior Corporate Manager/Executive:

Style:

My work type is ESTJ and my style is that of a "fact-minded, practical organizer." I like to organize people and projects and make sure that things are completed. My prime focus is on getting the job done. I have always been practical, realistic, and matter-of-fact, with a natural head for business and leadership. I like projects where the results of my work and my team's efforts are immediate, visible, and tangible. I can be tough when necessary, but I am also objective and logical. I am interested in having people around me who are entirely focused on getting the job done. I believe there should be rewards for meeting goals. I also enjoy community activities when they are meaningful and I have an opportunity to make an important contribution.

Career Type:

My primary career type is enterprising. I have always been drawn to a leadership role in any organization I have been in and consider myself aggressive and self-confident with good social and political skills. I prefer to work in a hard-driving, results-oriented environment with like-minded people. I communicate very effectively and have a wide network of professional colleagues and friends with whom I communicate regularly. My secondary career type is social. I am active in my community and enjoy working for useful causes. I like to use my leadership abilities to benefit others. I gravitate toward people who match my lifestyle and intellectual interests. My tertiary career type is conventional. I value economic achievement, material possessions, and status. I like my company to be well-organized with structured rules and to be a place where people are contributing to the overall success of the team.

Preferences:

I prefer most of the people with whom I work to be active, fast-moving, and energetic, interested in interacting with others regularly, well above average in skills and intelligence, and constantly pressing toward higher levels of achievement. I like to work in a hustling, bustling, large, open office in a modern building in the city. I would definitely like an assignment in Paris or London. I like to build and lead teams, deliver speeches, design systems, manage people, and manage my own investments. I expect my company to be tough, competitive, demanding, powerful, and influential.

Values and Needs:

I feel strongly about the following values and diligently maintain them in my worklife: leadership, status, power and authority, profit, gain, and high earnings. The values and needs that I feel are not yet satisfied in my worklife include nurturing and helping others, leisure, prestige and recognition, intellectual status, and adventure/excitement.

Functional Skills:

The skills at which I excel and which I feel have allowed me to be successful include acting assertively, influencing others, delegating responsibility, managing people, and making decisions. The functional skills that I am currently working on to improve in my worklife include understanding behavior, listening attentively, reading technical information, showing warmth and support, and writing creatively.

Adaptive Skills:

I consider the following adaptive skills as a source of strength: being challenge-seeking, imaginative, self-disciplined, resourceful, and a risk-taker. In order to round out my executive abilities, I need to be more encouraging of others, tolerant of others' mistakes, patient, versatile, and expressive.

Internal Barriers:

The following barriers have at times kept me from achieving all that I could and will need to be managed more consciously: all-or-nothing behavior, distrust of intuition, flexibility, sense of lack of creativity, and perfectionism.

Secretary:

Style:

My work type is ISFP and my style is that of an "observant, loyal helper." I am adaptable, caring, cooperative and loyal. I do not like disagreements. I am not interested in dominating or impressing other people. I like to work in a business situation where people are important and where the people I work with go about their business and enjoy it the way I do. I enjoy secretarial work because I can see the results of supporting my boss and working together as a team. I work best with a boss who understands me, lets me get my job done, and gives me some flexibility in completing my tasks. I also prefer to work in an environment that is reasonably quiet and well-ordered.

Career Type:

My primary career type is social. I am very interested in other people and sensitive to their needs. I like to understand people and help them. I do this both at work and at home with my family. Whenever I have had a choice about where to work I have always chosen a company or a department where people really get along together, are friendly, and help each other. This kind of place is most satisfying for me, and working there can be fun. My secondary career type is conventional. I like the structured, orderly environment of the office of an organized company with clear and well-defined rules and policies. I once worked in an architect's office where everything was very loose. Even though the people were friendly, I couldn't stand the disorganization and had to leave after three months. I am loyal and hardworking and can do a great job for a boss who really appreciates me. My tertiary career type is artistic. I like expressing myself through creative activities, including decorating, photography, and sketching with water colors. I like reading about art and architecture, and some of my friends are in the arts.

Preferences:

I really want to work around people who are well-organized, quick to show their emotions, fully self-expressive, friendly, and talkative about a wide variety of things, including subjects outside of work. I like to work best with a boss who is interested in my development, oriented to giving me significant challenges that stretch me, and highly interactive with my work. I want my workplace to be quiet and low-key, where I can use my own pictures and other things, preferably in a commercial office in the suburbs where I don't have to commute too far, and in a new building. I like to acquire new skills, act as a hostess, give personal advice, meet new people, and resolve conflicts among people. I prefer to work in a culture that is easygoing, small and friendly, well-organized, dedicated to a cause, and environmentally conscious.

Values and Needs:

The things that are most important to me and that I feel really strongly about keeping in my work and life are working with others, helping others, stability, exercising competence, and affiliation. The values and needs that I feel are not yet included enough in my worklife and that I would like to see better developed are achievement, adventure/excitement, helping society, community, and respect from others. I am working to include these things by doing more work as a volunteer and choosing what I think are very good causes to work for in my community.

Functional Skills:

The things I do best are serving others, showing warmth and support, working effectively on a team, taking quality photographs, and operating a computer terminal. I would like to develop more skill on my job in organizing information logically, evaluating data and ideas, influencing others, interviewing for information, and planning work assignments. I have always tried to develop myself by asking my boss to give me more responsibility and training wherever possible.

Adaptive Skills:

The personal qualities that are most important to me and that I think make me a good worker include being able to work well in a structured environment, being accurate, having integrity, being friendly, and being hardworking. I need to do better at being assertive, analytical, persistent, risk-taking, and tough-minded.

Internal Barriers:

My main barriers are difficulty selling myself, feelings of being unsophisticated, lack of assertiveness, being overly trusting, and lack of confidence.

Factory Worker:

Style:

My work type is ISTP and my style is that of a "practical analyzer." I don't like a line of bull! When people try to convince me of something, it needs to be logical. I like action, and I can work hard without getting tired. I am shy except with my family and best friends. I like working in a factory where things get done and everyone is focused on solving problems when they come up. I like to tell the truth about how I see things. I am very loyal to my friends and generous to my family.

Career Type:

My primary career type is realistic. I have good mechanical and athletic ability. I like concrete things like cars and boats and tools and good equipment. I prefer action to words. I like to produce useful things that are well made. I prefer working outdoors when I'm not in the factory. I have had some jobs outdoors, and they have been the best ones yet. My secondary career type is conventional. I like to be precise and well-organized, and to work in structured situations. I make friends slowly and have a small group of long-term close friends who have the same interests I do. My tertiary career type is social. I think more people should take responsibility for having their towns work better, including the schools and the police and other services. I am active in the local political club and like to have an influence on the way things get done. I also help raise money for the scouts and other groups for kids.

Preferences:

I want to work with people who are interested only in maintaining their own standards and leaving me to mine, who are practical and down-to-earth, and who are satisfied where they are and quietly productive. I like my supervisor to be at my level of knowledge and willing to let me do things my own way as long as the results are produced. I like to work outdoors or in a factory where everything has been put in place by the company and where the atmosphere is quiet and low-key. I like to install heavy equipment, operate assembly machinery, operate woodworking tools, repair things, and persuade others (especially about political issues). I like to work for a small and friendly, local, family-owned business, but one that is hard-driving and demanding.

Values and Needs:

The most important things to me are location, exercising competence, physical challenge, independence, and job tranquility. What I want more of is play, precision work, making decisions, respect from others, and status. To get these things, I would have to become a supervisor, which I have been avoiding because I am not sure I want too much responsibility at work that might interfere with the rest of my life.

Functional Skills:

The skills that I do best are assembling things, diagnosing mechanical problems, using power tools, following instructions, and thinking logically. If I want to be a supervisor I need to be able to lead others, manage people, motivate others, plan work assignments, and maintain schedules. I can take supervisory courses at work if I request them.

Adaptive Skills:

I am alert, conscientious, self-starting, physically strong, and industrious. I need to be more motivated, open to ideas, ambitious, encouraging of others, and people-oriented.

Internal Barriers:

I feel blocked by my fear of taking responsibility, being naive politically, having poor listening skills, being confrontational with others, and having a low frustration tolerance.

Independent Corporate Contributor:

Style:

My work type is INTP and my style is that of an "inquisitive analyzer." I am intensely analytical and objectively critical. I am mainly interested in ideas, very curious, and can't stand small talk. I learn very quickly, am insightful, intellectually curious, persevering, and thorough; and have sharply defined interests. I like an unstructured environment and like to work independently in solving thorny technical problems. I love logic and enjoy long, detailed arguments.

Career Type:

My primary career type is investigative. I am analytical and comfortable with abstractions, and prefer to cope with life and its problems by analytical thinking. I am scholarly and self-confident, and have scientific and mathematical ability. I like to work in a quiet and scholarly environment where I can pursue my work without interference and where there are plenty of intellectual resources like computers, laboratories, and libraries that I can use whenever I feel like it—night or day. My friends are mostly people I work with. My secondary career type is artistic. I play the piano and am a fairly competent amateur potter. I love music and feel a tremendous sense of self-expression when I am playing the piano or working with clay on my wheel. If I didn't have to make a living working in a company, I would stay at home and read, play music, and make pottery. That would make me very happy. None of the other career types seem to apply to me.

Preferences:

I want to work around people who are interested in getting their own work done without a lot of interaction with others, well above average in intelligence, focused in their conversations on their work, creatively disorganized, and inclined toward the intellectual. I prefer to work in a laboratory or library, in a private office, in my own home, or in any closed environment where I can concentrate on my work. I like to acquire new skills, classify and categorize information, invent new ways of doing things, perform laboratory experiments, and do library research. I prefer to work in a culture that is laissez-faire, intellectual, scientific, peaceful, and explorative.

Values and Needs:

The values and needs that are most important in my life, that are currently at a level that I find acceptable, and without which I would not be willing to work are creative expression, achievement, challenging problems, independence, and intellectual status. I definitely want more fame, prestige/recognition, variety, time freedom, and work on the frontiers of knowledge.

Functional Skills:

The areas where I really excel at work are analyzing facts and ideas, conceiving, creating, and developing ideas, gathering information and data, perceiving and defining cause-and-effect relationships, and synthesizing facts and ideas. The skills that I need to develop more are tuning in to needs and feelings of others, working effectively on a team, working within a structure, maintaining schedules, and following through. I think I need these because my growth as a contributor will require that I work more with others to develop and implement major projects.

Adaptive Skills:

The adaptive skills that work best for me are concentration, being demanding of myself, being intelligent, being methodical, and being a quick learner. In order to become more successful at creating and developing more important contributions, I will need to be more supportive of others, resilient, diplomatic, able to use time effectively, and empathetic.

Internal Barriers:

I need to handle the following barriers: difficulty managing time, becoming easily bored, impatience, being insensitive to the needs and feelings of others, and being stubborn.

Graduate Student:

Style:

My work type is ENTJ and my style is that of the "intuitive, innovative organizer." I have always enjoyed being a leader, taking charge, being assertive, and taking command of any situation I am in. I am well-informed, read a lot, and like to learn new things. I like to work around people who want to get things done, and I have little patience with inefficiency.

Career Type:

My primary career type is enterprising. I place a high value on political and economic matters and am drawn to power and leadership roles. I am assertive and self-confident. I like working with hard-driving people who are dedicated to achieving bottom-line results. I worked all through college in a student business and excelled at sales and marketing. I rose to the head of the business in my senior year and realized that I could have a good career in business as a leader or an executive. My secondary career type is investigative. I am analytical and comfortable with abstractions. I consider myself original in my thinking. I prefer strong intellectual discussions about things that interest me and avoid small talk unless it is politically useful. I gravitate toward people who match my lifestyle and interests. My tertiary career type is artistic. I like the theater, the opera, and the ballet. I spend time at museums and have taken several art history courses.

Preferences:

I want to be around people who are critical and demanding of excellence from themselves and me, well above average in intelligence, and able to turn out very large amounts of work day after day. I prefer a manager who is interested in my development and much more knowledgeable than me. I want to work in a medium-sized corporation in a modern office building in a big city and want to travel to other big cities in the United States and abroad. I want to acquire new skills, manage people, deliver speeches, lead teams, and solve organizational problems.

Values and Needs:

The values and needs that are most important to me and that I will be looking for on my first job are challenging problems, adventure/excitement, a fast pace, making decisions, and respect from others. The values and needs that I will be seeking as I get more experience in the business world include profit, power and authority, status, independence, and creative expression.

Functional Skills:

My most important functional skills are acting assertively, leading others, analyzing facts and ideas, presenting information logically, and understanding complex materials. The functional skills I think I need to work on to be successful in business are influencing others, relating to a wide variety of people, designing and developing systems, acknowledging the valuable contributions of others, and managing budgets.

Adaptive Skills:

My key personal qualities that I think will be valuable in my career include intelligence, being industrious, being aggressive, being goal-oriented, and having a strong will. I will need to improve myself in the areas of flexibility, being open to others, being considerate, being empathetic, and being able to admit mistakes.

Internal Barriers:

I want to eliminate these barriers that I think could inhibit my success in business: arrogance, being easily irritated, being slow to see humor, impatience, and inflexibility.

University Professor:

Style:

My work type is ENFJ and my style is that of an "imaginative harmonizer and worker with people." I am concerned with what others think or want and try to handle things with regard for other people's feelings. I am loyal to my institution and to people that I respect. I am a good teacher because I am at my best when speaking in front of groups. I put a lot of time into my work and am caring, tolerant, trustworthy, concerned and nurturing.

Career Type:

My primary career type is investigative. I am analytical and comfortable with abstractions, and prefer to handle problems through the use of analytical thinking. I consider myself to be highly original and have excellent verbal and mathematical skills. My secondary career type is social. I am a good teacher because I have a high interest in other people and am sensitive to their needs. I value interpersonal relations and use my social skills and verbal abilities to influence my students. My tertiary career type is artistic. I play the violin and spend time listening to music at home and going to concerts. I consider myself to be creative, expressive, and imaginative. I can express my ideas with emotion and strength and am a good writer.

Preferences:

I am best around people who are well above average in intelligence; friendly and talkative about a wide variety of things, including subjects outside of work; skeptical and questioning; willing to leave options open; and willing to let some piles grow on their desks. I like to work in a closed environment where I can concentrate on my work, in my own home or in a classroom or lecture hall on a university campus. I enjoy classifying and categorizing information, writing and delivering speeches and lectures, writing textbooks, and counseling students. I prefer to work in an organization that is permissive, peaceful, not-for-profit, privately owned, and committed to excellence.

Values and Needs:

The most important values and needs that are currently satisfied in my role as a faculty member at a prestigious university are achievement, creative expression, intellectual status, working on frontiers of knowledge, and independence. Those values and needs that I would most like to expand in my worklife include high earnings, helping society, artistic creativity, change and variety, and prestige and recognition. I am getting more of these values and needs into my life by writing a book and by attempting to expand the amount of consulting and lecturing that I do around the country.

Functional Skills:

My outstanding functional skills are teaching, communicating effectively, analyzing facts and ideas, presenting information logically, and playing a musical instrument. The functional skills that I would most like to improve for both work and pleasure include planning projects, managing budgets, criticizing constructively, operating a computer terminal, and maintaining physical stamina.

Adaptive Skills:

The adaptive skills that I think are most important to me and that are currently at an acceptable level are clear thinking, being independent, being intelligent, being tenacious, and being inventive. The most important adaptive skills that I think are currently in need of development include being able to deliver on time, being diplomatic, being politically aware, being organized, and being demanding of others.

Internal Barriers:

The following internal barriers should be reduced or eliminated: fear of financial insecurity, difficulty managing stress and pressure, being cynical and skeptical, impatience, and lack of diplomacy.

Human Resource Professional:

Style:

My work type is ENFP and my style is that of a "warmly enthusiastic planner of change." I am high-spirited, imaginative and able to do almost anything that interests me. I like to solve the problems that people have and am innovative and can see new ways of doing things. I have a lot of energy and initiative and use my feeling judgment to add depth to my insights. I like to work in an organization where there are not too many constraints, where my colleagues are imaginative, and where the work is concentrated on expanding human potential. I am a good networker and work hard to keep up with both friends and colleagues. I am sympathetic to others and have good insights into other people's personal problems.

Career Type:

My primary career type is social. I have a high interest in people and have based my career on working with people to help them improve their potential. My secondary career type is investigative. I am interested in analyzing things, although I would not want my whole job to be about facts and figures. I do have an analytical mind and like to use it in solving problems. I love a good intellectual discussion about things that interest me, especially when they concern how people behave at work and how that behavior can be modified or improved. My tertiary career type is enterprising. I am adventurous and persuasive. I am popular, assertive, and self-confident and enjoy leadership roles. I have lots of professional and personal relationships.

Preferences:

I prefer most of the people with whom I work to be interested in interacting with others regularly, quick to show their emotions and fully expressive, concerned and empathetic about me, helpful and companionable, and highly organized. I prefer to work indoors, in a suburban location, in a large, open office that is well equipped by the company, and in an environment with windows looking out on an interesting view. The kind of work I like includes coaching work teams, counseling people with substance abuse problems, giving personal advice, planning projects, and resolving conflicts among people. I like a large corporation that is competitive, iconoclastic, growing rapidly, and influential.

Values and Needs:

The most important values and needs that are currently satisfied in my worklife include knowledge, helping others, working with others, exercising competence, and independence. The values and needs that are currently not fully satisfied and that I would like to include in my life are challenging problems, advancement, prestige and recognition, helping society, and high earnings.

Functional Skills:

The functional skills that I use the most on my job and that I enjoy using are motivating others, tuning in to the needs and feelings of others, training people, coordinating events and operations, and presenting information logically. The functional skills that I would most like to improve are promoting ideas, managing conflict, maintaining schedules, understanding complex materials, and writing creatively. Improving these skills would allow me to be a more independent producer of results.

Adaptive Skills:

My most important adaptive skills currently at an acceptable level are being purposeful, dedicated to personal goals, dependable, spontaneous, and people-oriented. I need development in self-discipline, being firm, being a risk-taker, being challenge-seeking, and being systematic.

Internal Barriers:

The internal barriers that most inhibit my success include conflicting values, fear of looking foolish, low stress tolerance, being overly trusting, and being restless.

Inconsistencies and the Uses of Uncertainty

If you read the first example (starting on page 92) carefully, you will have noticed some inconsistencies between the various sections. For instance, in the section on career types, the writer (a male) says that he considers himself aggressive and self-confident. Yet, in the section on internal barriers, he says that lack of assertiveness is a key barrier that he needs to work on for more satisfaction and success. These seemingly contradictory statements point to an important function of the Personal Career Profile. They prove human beings are not entirely consistent in their behavior *or* in their understanding of themselves and others. No matter how sophisticated or comprehensive an assessment appears to be, people's thoughts, actions, and feelings are never *entirely* predictable. But where inconsistencies arise, they signal areas of uncertainty. These require further exploration and thought, and where they occur, you are encouraged to delve deeper. You may wish to read some of the additional materials suggested in previous chapters; spend more time thinking about the issues involved; review some of the assessments you did in this book; discuss your profile with friends, family, peers, subordinates, your boss, or others who know you well; or even try counseling or therapy.

Using Your Detailed Profile

This detailed Career Profile will increase your self-awareness, self-esteem, and self-acceptance, and support you in making decisions. The detailed statement will be useful to you whenever you prepare for performance or development meetings with your manager. It should be central to your own career development planning—whether independently or in a formal course, program, or workshop. It can further assist you in planning a development program or in planning a career or job change. Your *Personal Career Profile*® will be invaluable in the preparation of résumés and job interviews.

9

THE CAREER DISCOVERY PROJECT: MANAGING YOUR CAREER

If you completed all of the exercises in this book, you probably discovered great satisfaction in knowing more about yourself. In addition to this subjective benefit, all the information developed in these exercises will be useful in managing your career—in selecting a career for yourself, planning your career path, advancing your career, changing careers, determining the development you need to follow a specific career, moving into a new job that fits you well, or improving your performance and satisfaction in your current job.

Exploring Appropriate Career Options

You can start by recognizing the patterns that exist in the relationships between the various assessments and inventories. The patterns may suggest the kinds of work environments that would be most appropriate for you to explore. Here are some of the questions you can ask yourself as you look through your Concise or Detailed Personal Career Profiles:

- *Does the relationship between my work type and my career type suggest a pattern?*

  For example, people who have an intuitive-thinking work type (NT) and an investigative career type (I) might consistently find themselves drawn toward jobs in which abstract thinking and problem-solving play a significant role. They might be unhappy in a work situation without sufficient challenge to their deductive thinking processes.

- *Does the relationship between my work type and my adaptive skills suggest a pattern?*

  People with a sensing-perceiving work type (SP) and adaptive skills that include such items as "service-oriented," "sensitive to others," "dependable," "energetic," and "people-oriented" might find great satisfaction in a position where they can spend their time supporting and serving people, helping people overcome difficulties, and in general working in the service of and in direct contact with others. They would probably be dissatisfied on an assembly line or in the back office in an administrative position.

- *Does the relationship between my career type and my most important functional (people, data, and physical) skills suggest a pattern?*

  People with an enterprising career type (E) and a dominance of physical rather than people or data functional skills would probably be most satisfied running their own business where they have an opportunity to use their hands in repairing things, manufacturing machine parts, moving furniture, or installing machinery. It might be inappropriate for them to become consultants, operate a real estate franchise, or run a business that has major interactions with people and information.

- *Does the relationship between my functional skills and my internal barriers suggest a pattern?*

  People with a dominance of data functional skills and internal barriers that suggest difficulty in relating well to people would probably find more satisfaction in an independent contributor role, doing research or other kinds of analytic work in an environment without too much interaction with others.

It is also instructive to look over each of your four preference lists in Chapter 2 and write down the patterns that emerge as you study them. Some of the questions you might ask yourself as you look through these lists include:

- *Do the kinds of people I prefer to work with indicate that I really want to work around people, or would I prefer to spend more time working by myself?*

- *Do I prefer a very specific kind of physical environment, or can I be satisfied almost anywhere as long as the people, job, and culture are right?*

- *Are there a wide range of jobs I would enjoy doing, or are the jobs limited to a specific few?*

- *In which specific kind of work culture would I be most satisfied?*

Listing your top five preferences side-by-side, as you did in the Concise Personal Career Profile, will also allow you to discover the patterns of preferences that point toward specific jobs and careers.

Mastering Your Current Job

If you are in a job, good career management starts where you are right now. Reading through your completed assessments will help you determine whether your job is consistent with your style, preferences, values and needs, skills, and internal barriers. Through this examination, you can take the steps necessary to include in your job the factors that contribute to your satisfaction. Conversely, you'll be able to trace sources of job dissatisfaction and discover ways to reduce the disparity between you and your current work environment. In addition, you can create a plan to satisfy the developmental needs you discovered and work toward being more effective in your job. If you ask for your boss's support in implementing your development plan, you'll identify yourself as a responsible and thoughtful employee—a person of greater value to the organization.

Advancing Your Career

The assessments are also useful for planning your career advancement. Pay particular attention to your developmental needs, especially in the area of skills and internal barriers. Compare your skills with those required for the jobs you want to move into. Make sure your developmental list is focused toward where you want to go. If you want to move up to a management position, find out which functional and adaptive skills make the best manager and start to work on any deficiencies you may have. Make sure you are willing to eliminate, or at least reduce, any internal barriers that could stand in your way of being a successful manager. Find out if your style is consistent with the preferred management style in your organization. If not, what can you do to adapt and change? If you are not willing to adapt and change, are you willing to deal with the barriers that will inevitably arise as you try to climb the ladder?

Making a Career Change

At some time or other in your life—maybe more than once—it may become appropriate for you to change careers. Perhaps the choice will be entirely your own. Or, changing circumstances may provide the opportunity. However it comes about, a career change is a major turning point in your life and should be thought through carefully. The assessments will be particularly useful in looking at alternative career decisions. It is most important to compare the work environment characteristics of the new career with the preferences you selected in Chapter 2. It is also important to make sure that the values and needs you selected in Chapter 7 will be satisfied in a new career. The following example will illustrate the benefits to be gained from careful examination of the assessments and *Profile*.

Beverly Carlson was an administrative manager in a large corporation and was reasonably satisfied in her job until the recession hit. Her company was badly affected and started to reduce staff. By the summer of 1991 she had started to lose sleep over the rising insecurity in her job. Many of her colleagues had been fired, and she guessed it would only be a matter of months before she would get her notice.

Two years earlier, Beverly had gone through a career management workshop sponsored by her company. The results of the assessment she did in that program are documented in Chapter 8 (see the Detailed Personal Career Profile for the Corporate Administrator starting on page 94).

Beverly realized in reading over her profile that she needed and wanted a stable, secure position working in a quiet, low-key office among people who would let her get her work done to her own standards. She was also aware that her current job did not satisfy her need for intellectual status, leisure, and the ability to work alone. She knew, from her reading of the financial section of her local paper, that many other corporations were having the same problems as hers. She also knew that small accounting firms and other small, entrepreneurial businesses were on the rise. Because her style was that of an "analytical manager of facts and details," she would probably be very useful in this environment. She could command the respect and independence she desired and get the flexibility she needed to satisfy her time freedom and leisure needs.

Beverly concentrated her job search on the smaller companies in her area— commercial businesses, accounting firms, financial planners, and others that might need her organizational and financial skills. Before she could be laid off, she landed a position in a five-year-old manufacturing business that was growing very rapidly. It needed someone with corporate experience to serve as its comptroller and act as the chief link with its clients' financial people as well as with its accounting firm. Beverly is excited and challenged in her new position and is glad she made the switch.

An Enduring Reference Tool

However you choose to use the information derived from this battery of assessments and inventories, recognize the work you've done here as a sound foundation on which to build a more satisfying worklife. Knowing as much about yourself as you now do will enable you to answer all sorts of questions that arise as you claim greater control over your own career.

Refer back to the work you've done and to your *Personal Career Profile*® whenever you have a question about the quality of your worklife or the direction of your career, and to allay doubts about job or career choices you may be about to make. Continue to manage your career toward greater satisfaction and improved performance. The rewards will inevitably follow.

10

SUGGESTIONS FOR FURTHER READING

The field of self-assessment and its relation to people's work has received significant attention from hundreds of authors. Considering the importance of the issues involved, surprisingly few books in the field have made it to any kind of bestseller list. Those described below are a small sample of what is available, but enough to give you a deeper appreciation of the purposes of the assessments you've carried out in this book.

Style

An enormous amount has been written about psychological type and style, particularly in connection with the Myers-Briggs Type Indicator,® in the format of books, pamphlets, Ph.D. theses, technical papers and journal articles, and proprietary consulting documents. A few of the more accessible and useful materials are described here. All contain an abundance of references if you wish to delve deeper in this area.

1. *Introduction to Type: A Description of the Theory and Applications of the Myers-Briggs Type Indicator*, by Isabel Briggs Myers, Consulting Psychologists Press, fourth edition, 1987. This thirty-two-page booklet contains an excellent introduction to the theory of types and a detailed, readable discussion of each of the types and styles. A short section is included on applications of type and style in relationships and career choices, the effects of each preference in work situations, and the use of type to improve problem solving.

2. *Introduction to Type in Organizational Settings*, by Sandra Krebs Hirsh and Jean M. Kummerow, Consulting Psychologists Press, 1987. Another thirty-two-page booklet, containing brief descriptions of the sixteen types with material on preferences in work situations, preferred methods of communication, contributions to organizations, leadership style, preferred work environment, and potential pitfalls, plus suggestions for development.

3. *Please Understand Me: Character and Temperament Types*, by David Keirsey and Marilyn Bates, distributed by Prometheus Nemesis Book Company, published by Gnosology Books, fourth edition, 1984. A readable, interesting, and informative paperback dealing with a variety of issues concerning psychological type and style. It includes the Keirsey Temperament Sorter, another assessment tool that leads to a determination of the sixteen psychological types, which are described at length. Style is discussed with respect to life-mates, temperament in children, and temperament in leading, but less extensively with regard to career, job preferences, and work style.

4. *Gifts Differing*, by Isabel Briggs Myers with Peter B. Myers, Consulting Psychologists Press, 1980. In paperback format, this warm and moving book describes the history of the work of Katharine Briggs and her daughter, Isabel Briggs Myers, in the extension of Jungian typology and the development of the MBTI.® The sixteen types are described in considerable detail, and the complementary nature of preferences and types is extremely well developed. A chapter on type and occupation discusses the relationship of each type to worklife. Applications are discussed in further chapters on use of the opposites, type and marriage, type and early learning, and learning styles.

5. *People Types and Tiger Stripes: A Practical Guide to Learning Styles*, by Gordon Lawrence, Center for Applications of Psychological Type, second edition, 1982. A 100-page paperback that includes *Introduction to Type* (see reference 1 above), this book probes the relationship between type and learning styles, including materials on using types in planning instruction, developmental needs and type concepts, type and teaching styles, and type and learning styles.

6. *Type Talk*, by Otto Kroeger and Janet Thuesen, Delacorte Press, 1988. The authors have developed a popular guide on how to understand your personality type, with applications to your worklife and your personal and parent/child relationships.

Career Type (Holland Typology)

The Holland typology (R-I-A-S-E-C) has also received tremendous attention. There is hardly a publication on jobs or careers that does not at least mention the typology. Most use it extensively. Only a few of the many books treating career types are mentioned here. They in turn will lead you to more if you care to dig deeper.

1. *Making Vocational Choices: A Theory of Careers*, by John L. Holland, Prentice-Hall, 1985. An expanded revision of Holland's original 1966 *The Psychology of Vocational Choice*, this book explains how the typology was developed and includes both theoretical and practical considerations.

2. *Coming Alive from Nine to Five: The Career Search Handbook*, by Betty Neville Michelozzi, Mayfield Publishing Company, third edition, 1988. An extremely thorough, 300-page, large-format paperback that deals in depth with the subject of job motivation. Includes dozens of inventories, exercises, and other materials that help the reader to discover his or her "job satisfiers." The discussion of the Holland types is outstanding. The book also includes excellent chapters on job-finding and the job market for the nineties.

3. *Taking Charge of Your Career Direction*, by Robert D. Lock, Brooks/Cole Publishing Company (Wadsworth, Inc.), 1988. This 375-page, large-format paperback has the depth and detail of a textbook and contains assessments and exercises. It includes tables of educational majors classified by Holland types and further information about jobs and careers with respect to the types. Contains a particularly fine discussion of work values.

4. *If You Don't Know Where You're Going, You'll Probably End Up Somewhere Else*, by David Campbell, Ph.D., Argus Communications, 1974. This 144-page, pocket-sized paperback can be read in one easy sitting and is filled with amusing drawings, one-liners, and an effective message about lifework planning. The section on the Holland types is succinct and informative.

5. *Dictionary of Holland Occupational Codes*, compiled by Gary D. Gottfredson, John L. Holland, and Deborah Kimiko Ogawa, Consulting Psychologists Press, 1989. Almost 500 pages in a paperback format, this massive volume contains a comprehensive cross-index of Holland types with twelve thousand occupations from the *Dictionary of Occupational Titles*. Contains a detailed bibliography of materials on occupational research and applications.

Skills Identification

1. *The Three Boxes of Life, and How to Get Out of Them*, by Richard N. Bolles, Ten Speed Press, 1981. By America's best-known author on careers and jobs, this paperback volume of almost 500 pages provides a stimulating exploration of the art and technology of creating a balanced life. It contains good job-search material and an excellent section on the Holland types and their relationship to work and specific occupations. The same author and publisher have provided *What Color Is Your Parachute?* and *Where Do I Go From Here With My Life?*

2. *The New Quick Job-Hunting Map*, by Richard N. Bolles, Ten Speed Press, 1989. This highly readable and usable pamphlet contains an excellent group of skill-identification exercises treating functional, specific content, and adaptive skills.

3. *Your Hidden Skills*, by Henry C. Pearson, Moury Press, 1981. Shows you how to identify the skills you already possess but are not fully aware of. Twelve clearly defined steps (with forms) help you develop a pattern of your key talents. The process also proves that you already use them effectively. Based on a system initiated at Polaroid Corporation and developed by the author over a seven-year period in both corporate and noncorporate settings.

4. *The Complete Job-Search Handbook*, by Howard Figler, Ph.D., Henry Holt and Company, 1988. Figler is one of the most articulate writers in the career field. This excellent paperback of almost 400 pages contains discussions and exercises on motivation, values, and skills. His work on values is particularly good, and the discussion of skills is outstanding.

5. *Guerrilla Tactics in the Job Market*, by Tom Jackson, Bantam Books, 1991. A classic in the field of job search. Contains excellent exercises for translating skills and interests into meaningful job and career targets.

General Career Planning

1. *The Salaried Professional: How to Make the Most of Your Career*, Joseph A. Raelin, Praeger Publishers, 1984. This detail-packed paperback of almost 300 pages is one of the few books to treat the multiple relationships among psychological type, motivation, career types, values, skills, and the other indicators of people's relationship to their worklives. Fully referenced, it includes inventories and exercises useful to career exploration, learning how to excel in a job, and effectively managing and developing a career.

2. *Taking Charge of Your Career Direction*, by Robert D. Lock, Brooks/Cole Publishing Company, 1988. Highly readable and thorough, this book contains an excellent set of inventories and exercises on interests, skills, motivations, and work values. Several chapters show you how to clarify your occupational prospects, make career decisions, and test the reality of your career choice.

3. *The Inventurers: Excursions in Life and Career Renewal*, by Janet Hagber and Richard Leider, Addison-Wesley Publishing Company, 1982. You're an "inventurer" if you are "willing to take a long look at yourself and consider new options, venture inward, and explore." This unusual book takes a holistic approach to career planning, including mind, body, and spirit. Contains material on life stages and styles, work styles, and a formatted process for making choices about these critical issues, including exercises and inventories.

4. *Your Career: Choices, Chances, Changes*, by David C. Borchard, John J. Kelly, and Nancy Pat K. Weaver, Kendall Hunt Publishing Company, 1984. A 300-page, large-format paperback, this comprehensive workbook contains a full career planning process, including inventories, assessments, and exercises. Also suggests ways to organize small discussion groups and conduct career information interviews, and contains other activities useful to both the career planner and the career facilitator, instructor, or counselor.

5. *Altered Ambitions*, by Betsy Jaffe, Ed.D., Donald I. Fine, 1991. Exercises and questionnaires pinpoint your personal style of coping with change and show how to focus on your own patterns and priorities, develop new skills, and plan a career path tailored to your needs. Shows how a tough employment market and corporate restructuring require flexibility, willingness to alter career ambitions, and new approaches to balancing the demands of workplace and family.

6. *The Career Doctor*, by Neil M. Yeager, Ed.D., John Wiley and Sons, 1991. Teaches you to diagnose and treat such problems as burnout, lack of confidence, workaholism, unrealizable expectations, office politics, and others.

7. *Managing Your Career with Power*, by Gerald M. Sturman, Ph.D., Bierman House, 1990. Complete career management guide, including text and exercises leading to a complete personal development plan.

8. *Out the Organization*, by Madeleine Swain and Robert Swain, Mastermedia, 1989. The career management book for professionals whose careers are no longer satisfying or safe. Shows you how to launch your own career plan with pragmatic, realistic courses of action.

Management Development

1. *Successful Manager's Handbook: Development Suggestions for Today's Manager*, edited by Brian L. Davis, Ph.D., Lowell W. Hellervik, Ph.D., and James L. Sheard, Ph.D., Personnel Decisions, third edition, 1989. This large-format paperback of over 450 pages may comprise some of the best material of its kind publicly available, with extremely detailed personal-development exercises, tips, and advice for anyone who aspires to become an excellent manager. Administrative, leadership, interpersonal, communication, and cognitive skills are all covered in detail, as are personal adaptability, personal motivation, and occupational/technical knowledge.

2. *Social Skills*, by Robert Bolton, Touchstone Books, 1986. This communication handbook uncovers roadblocks to successful communication and treats the ability to listen, self-assertion, conflict resolution, and working out problems with others. Both thought-provoking and practical, it is full of ideas that you can use to improve your communication in meaningful ways.

3. *High Performance Leadership—Strategies for Maximum Productivity*, by Philip Harris, Scott Foresman and Company, 1989. The author is a behavioral psychologist and top management consultant. In this book, he provides an in-depth exploration of the managerial skills required to create a maximum-performance environment. Includes a wealth of ideas and resources enabling managers to develop necessary skills for coping with changing organizations.

4. *Social Style/Management Style: Developing Productive Working Relationships*, by Robert Bolton and Dorothy Grover Bolton, Amacom Books, American Management Association, 1984. Are you an Amiable, an Analytical, an Expressive, or a Driver? This book shows you how to recognize your particular management style and use it to manage others more effectively, increase creativity, and set appropriate life goals.

5. *Straight Talk for Monday Morning*, by Allan Cox, John Wiley and Sons, 1990. One hundred real-life stories identify the personal qualities that evoke the best responses from people—qualities that can transform a manager into a leader. Each story offers a moral that can be put into actions that get results.

Internal Barriers—Personal Growth and Development

Although books like those discussed below are no substitute for working with a professional counselor or therapist on internal barriers, they can raise the level of your awareness, expand your perspective, and provide useful strategies and techniques for coping more effectively with barriers.

1. *Your Perfect Right*, by Robert E. Alberti and Michael Emmons, Impact Publishers, 1988. This book is a classic in the assertiveness-training field. This totally revised and expanded edition includes excellent chapters on goal-setting and on-the-job assertiveness. This book can help you to express yourself positively and respect others at the same time.

2. *The Plateauing Trap*, by Judith Bardwick, Bantam Books, 1986. Do you ever feel as if your career is at a standstill—that your work has lost its challenge and your life has become a tedious routine? If so, your worklife can be described as *plateaued*. The author, a psychologist and leading management consultant, discusses how to escape being stuck on this plateau and revitalize your career. Practical strategies will enable you to create a fresh opportunity for personal growth and positive change. Includes an excellent discussion on balancing your personal and professional life.

3. *Feeling Good—the New Mood Therapy*, by David D. Burns, Wukkuan Morris and Co., 1980. This is the first major book introducing the principles of cognitive therapy to the general public. It teaches us that by changing the way we think about things, we can alter our moods, deal with emotionally upsetting problems, and reduce depression and anxiety. The author outlines a systematic program for controlling thought distortions that lead to pessimism, low self-esteem, anger, guilt, and other common difficulties of daily living. The book includes an excellent discussion of ways to overcome perfectionism.

4. *Overcoming Procrastination*, by Albert Ellis and William Knaus, NAL Penguin Co., 1977. One of the first and best books to help people understand why they procrastinate and to develop strategies and tactics for dealing with the problem. The book uses the techniques of rational emotive therapy, combining cognitive, behavioral, and emotive methods for overcoming procrastination.

5. *When Smart People Fail*, by Carol Hyatt and Linda Gottlieb, Penguin Group, 1980. Positive reassurance that defeats are not only survivable—they can be stepping-stones for renewed success. This book focuses solely on career failure. It shows you how to cope with setbacks and take advantage of options and sets out the nine most common reasons for failure—poor interpersonal skills, mismatch of abilities, mismatch of personalities, mismatch of styles, mismatch of values, lack of commitment, sex discrimination, race discrimination, and age discrimination.

6. *Self-Esteem*, by Matt McKay and Pat Fanning, St. Martin's Press, 1987. This book provides a valuable discussion of tactics and strategies for rebuilding your self-esteem. It includes material to help you discover which of your "personal rules" and "shoulds" are healthy and which cause conflict, guilt, and negative reactions.

7. *Overcoming Indecisiveness*, by Theodore Rubin, Harper and Row, 1985. Rubin describes a step-by-step plan of attack on indecisiveness that can strengthen your sense of self. Provides useful ideas and strategies for anyone having trouble making up his or her mind.

8. *Taking Care of Business—a Psychiatrist's Guide for True Career Success*, by David Viscott, Pocket Books, 1985. The better you manage yourself and others, the more you'll succeed in your career. In this humane and down-to-earth guide, Dr. Viscott shows you how to develop the personal insights and communication skills vital to achieving your professional goals. Powerful techniques are provided to help you read people clearly, recognize your own talents, and negotiate successfully. A particularly useful section is the discussion on how to recognize three main personality types—dependent, controlling, and competitive—and how to respond to each constructively.

9. *How to Be Organized in Spite of Yourself*, by Sunny Schlesenger and Roberta Roesch, NAL Books, 1989. This is an excellent book dealing with time management, space management, improving organization, and reducing clutter. The authors have devised personalized solutions providing ten different systems to match ten distinct personality types.

10. *Making Therapy Work: Your Guide to Choosing, Using, and Ending Therapy*, by Fredda Bruckner-Gordon, Barbara K. Gangi, and Geraldine Wallman, Harper and Row, 1988. For all those considering working with a professional therapist, this is a hands-on guide to getting the most out of individual, group, or family counseling. The authors provide basic consumer information for finding the right kind of psychotherapy for you, including how to choose among different schools of therapy. The book also discusses such topics as taking stock of your life, building a good working relationship with your therapist, overcoming obstacles to change, and knowing what to do when someone you care about needs help. A rich resource section is included with recommended readings, referral organizations, and hot lines.

11. *You Don't Have to Go Home from Work Exhausted*, by Ann McGee-Cooper, Pfeiffer and Company, 1991. Personalized how-to guide for energizing work habits, thinking patterns, work environment, morning routine, commute time, evening and weekend playtime, relationships, and your overall approach to life. Contains action items, anecdotes, quotes, and techniques for increasing creativity.

12. *Dinosaur Brains*, by Albert J. Bernstein and Sydney Craft Rozen, John Wiley and Sons, 1991. Analyses of office politics and conflicts at work as well as strategies for handling problem bosses and subordinates, manipulators, angry customers, self-promoters, the old-boy network, mentors, and more. Includes step-by-step instructions for coping with difficult people and improving job performance.